Teen Investing Guide

The Ultimate Young Person's Guide to Save, Invest, and Build Wealth In 6 Easy Steps

Will D. Harris

Table of Contents

Introduction

One of the reasons why poor people are sometimes considered happier than the rich is because they do not have to deal with the guilt and self-blame that comes from the poor handling of funds. Many times, money "passes" through our coffers than stays. The art of saving and planning the use of money is essential and is key to finding peace in life. This should be instilled in our lives at a very young age so that even when we are old, we will look back and smile at our financial journey. It is a good thing never to have to worry about money because you will have amassed enough to cover your needs. It is everyone's dream to achieve financial freedom earlier, rather than later.

It is often said that money—whatever the amount—can never be enough, but there sure should be a ceiling to that statement. Some simple things can be done today to better your financial situation tomorrow. It is unfortunate that most people only realize this late, when many years have been wasted and there isn't much that can be done to better the situation. This book is meant to teach young people to manage their finances and to build sizable financial knowledge from a very young age. One needs to have a reasonable understanding of financial management at a very young age. It is the foundation on which you build financial liberty in years to come.

Sources of income differ from individual to individual. Some people get into jobs at very young ages and have paychecks coming in. Some may be earning dividends, getting royalties, and other varying sources of income. At a young age, the urge is usually to spend the money and to live "the life." While that may be the 'in thing", being wise with your money helps you in the long run. The future depends on today. If you are that young person who does not only want to marvel at rich people but to be one of them, this book is the perfect companion for you.

This book is not only a mirror through which you see yourself in the future but a handy informant on how to get there. Dreaming alone is not enough. One has to act to bring the dream to fruition. The guidelines in this book will help you to start acting today for the life you want to live tomorrow. You do not want to look back at your young life and say, "If only I had known." Here is the companion you need to be wise with your money and build wealth.

You will also learn from this book how money works, and how you need to watch your spending patterns. The urge to overspend and to splash finances is quite high at a young age because when we are young, we hardly ever think of how our actions shape the future. If you can overcome the reckless spending of money at a young age, you stand a greater chance at financial liberty in the future. This book is therefore the number one tool in helping you to personally manage your finances—as little as they are. You wouldn't want to wait until you amass a big sum of money to start learning how to manage it. This is a bad idea because you may never be able to do so. You have to start small and gradually build towards your financial liberty.

The book will cover several areas that I consider vital to financial wisdom. It will start by explaining budgeting in detail. Whenever you handle money, you should plan on how it will be used. Budgeting teaches you to prioritize and keep track of your spending patterns. The book will however mainly focus on investment, an art that will help you to amass wealth from the little you have. This is because when you have money at hand, you should not only think of allocating uses to it but rather growing it to be enjoyed later. Never live from hand to mouth but rather learn to set aside money for future use. The book shall help you to understand the value of money and to create value for yourself. This is a lot of good stuff to take in, so let's get straight into the flesh of wealth creation through budgeting and investment.

Chapter 1:

Budget

This chapter covers probably the most important aspect of money handling. A budget is an estimated account of income and expenditure for a certain period of time, for example, a month. An individual who has a certain source of income can always have a budget for themselves. A budget clearly outlines the uses to which money is allocated. It can be based on estimated income or on actual income depending on whether or not income is known. With estimated income, you are assuming that you will get a certain income at the end of the time period. The actual income you end up getting may be plus or minus the estimated, but that will not affect your budgeting goal.

Figure 1: Budgeting is important.

Types of Budgets

Budgeting will help you keep track of your spending patterns and brings you the peace of mind that comes from knowing you are in control of your finances. There are three types of budgets that can be implemented by an individual. These are the balanced budget, the surplus budget, and the deficit budget.

The Balanced Budget

A balanced budget is one where the estimated expenditure is equal to the estimated revenue. This means that you plan on spending everything you earn and there is literally no room for savings. This is a dangerous form of budgeting. It does not ensure financial stability for an individual. In most cases, you will end up on the negative because unexpected expenses that have not been budgeted for may creep up. Out of your income, you will not have any room to cover those expenses and you will be forced to look to alternative sources of funds—like credit. This budget is not the best option for an individual with a developmental mindset who has the insight to grow themselves financially. Your pocket should always have breathing space.

Saving is a difficult thing to do. You must bear in mind that you should save before you spend. It should never be the opposite. If you have not yet saved out of your income, then you should halt your spending until you have set apart your savings. Teach yourself this principle. To help the situation, you can automate transfers from your checking account into your savings account. That way, you cannot overspend and encroach on the money that should be saved. Make it a point to save, then spend. This will help you to avoid always being one paycheck from broke. The saving before spending approach works for every income level.

Saving is like hiding money so that you do not spend it on things you do not necessarily need. Whenever you want to spend money on something you do not need, or can survive without, think twice and transfer that money into your savings account. Grow it first, and spend it later. To make it easier, you should have two bank accounts. One is for savings, and the other for cash flow. The cash flow account is the first account into which your regular income lands. This regular income refers to dividends, royalties, or your paycheck. Once the cash flow account receives income, you have to transfer a certain percentage to the savings account depending on the expenses you have to cover that month. For example, if you receive $1,000 into your checking account, you can immediately transfer $200 into your savings account. You will not be able to use this money because you will not have a card to use.

Save first, and spend even up to the last cent of the money in your cash flow account. Many people will say their income is not enough to cater for saving because they need to use all of it to survive. This is not true. You can always tighten your expenses and learn to survive with what you have, just like you would if your salary was reduced. You would take it upon yourself to make your income work for you while taking care of your saving needs. You must see your savings account growing every year. If you make it a point to save a certain amount of money every month, your account will grow constantly. In the example given above, at the end of the year, you will have at least $2,400 in your savings account. You need to see your bank account growing more and more.

Your savings bank account has to be enough to fund at least 12 months of your lifestyle. If you spend $800 every month, your savings must be at least $9,600. The more money you have, the more powerful and confident you feel. You will enjoy peace of mind. Whenever you have an emergency, you do not enter into panic mode because you have savings to help you out.

The Surplus Budget

When your estimated income exceeds your estimated expenditure, this is a surplus budget. After all the expenses have been covered, the budget leaves some extra money that can be invested or saved. This type of budget can be the lead-up to wealth creation. Most people work and earn money so that they are just able to get by. If you earn enough to take care of your needs and have some change in your pocket, you have to be wise with the change. Most people have the idea that if they have extra money, it is an indication that they may increase their expenses or make life more luxurious. Reality is not so. The perfect mindset would see the opportunity to invest once there is some extra money.

The surplus budget is the most ideal budget for a young person who wants to create wealth. This is because it teaches one to be in control of their expenditure and to invest money so that it grows into better income tomorrow. One should cut back on spending, do away with unnecessary expenses, and create more space for saving and investment. Remember, the more surplus you have in your budget, the higher the amount you can invest and the higher the returns from the investment.

The Deficit Budget

When the estimated expenditure exceeds the estimated income, this is a deficit budget. This means that there is a shortfall in your income. I always discourage this kind of budgeting technique because it leads one astray. You should always live within your means. Do not spend what you do not have, but rather ensure that you can cover your expenses out of what you earn.

Spending Less Than You Earn

Guina (2019) states that spending less is more than cutting costs, it is peace of mind. You avoid living a paycheck to paycheck existence when you start spending less than you earn. The stress that comes from living income to income is something you wouldn't want to live with. It is up to you to live a stress-free life. You owe that to yourself. When you spend less than you earn, you can invest for your future and have alternative sources of income coming in. It is the foundation of wealth creation. Unless you learn to save, you cannot grow financially. Make it a habit to use "some" of your money, not all of it; then put the remainder to good use. The question most of us may now have is, "How do I spend less than I earn?" Let us look into that.

How to Spend Less Than You Earn

It is a fact that everyone has some sort of income, whether from a job or allowances and maybe pocket money. This means that everyone can afford to invest if ever they want to. It is not true that you should have a big income to be able to save. Saving small sums of money periodically will eventually add up to a sizable figure. You need to make some small changes to your lifestyle that will have a lasting impact on your life. Here are some tips on how you can get yourself to spend less than you earn.

Cut Back on Expenses

Let us assume that out of your monthly income you have to pay for some expenses that you cannot forego. The first idea that comes to mind whenever we hear of cutting back on expenses is to get whatever we have always paid for at cheaper prices. The best way to cut back is not to bargain, but to avoid incurring the expense at all. For example, if you are in the habit of buying lunch every day, try taking a packed lunch instead of buying a cheaper lunch. That is one less expense. Try to determine what cheaper alternative you have to your current expense. You should also look into your expenses to determine which ones you can do without. Consider cutting back on luxurious expenses, like manicures and pedicures. Some of these things can be foregone today to be enjoyed tomorrow.

Have an Emergency Fund

An emergency fund helps you to cover unexpected expenses without having to overspend or enter into debt. This fund is some sort of savings that you keep so that when need be, it helps beef up your disposable money and leaves your budget at a surplus. The idea is simple, you do not have to use your current earnings to cover unnecessary expenses. Imagine this. You walk into a shop with fragile goods and accidentally break something. This was obviously unbudgeted for. The emergency fund will come in to take care of the situation whilst your budget still has breathing space.

Study Your Financial Habits

You can make use of, say, a notebook to keep track of every time you spend your money. This helps you to track your spending and determine where you need to adjust. Many of the times we handle money, it just blows through our hands and we cannot account for where it went. For every cent spent, have a recording. At the end of the month, group your expenses and add them up. You will be surprised. For example, you may then realize that you spent quite an amount on chewing gum. That is not a necessity and you may have thought of it as a small amount that will not affect your budget much. However, those small amounts put together will add up to an amount that you will later realize ate into your finances. You should therefore study your spending habits and make necessary adjustments.

Create a Budget

After having taken the time to study your spending habits, you will be able to make a budget for yourself. You have a clear picture of what your recurring expenses are. These are those that you encounter every month. This can easily be budgeted for because you know they will surely come. You can then also budget for unexpected expenses if you do not have an emergency fund. This is a wise move because you will have considered any uncertainties or emergencies and still have a surplus. Should there be no arisings, the money set aside for unexpected expenses can add to the savings of that month. That is wise, isn't it? Always budget for your money. That way, you will be able to spend less than you earn.

These tips will help you to have controlled expenditure. You will not believe the satisfaction and peace of mind that comes from being responsible with your money and from being practical about your future spending needs. The future is made now, so learning and mastering these habits at an early age is something you really want to do. We have so far discussed the importance of having a budget, but you probably have never seen a budget before. Let us now look at how you can create the budget.

How to Create a Personal Budget

As explained earlier, having a budget helps you control your spending as well as keep track of your income. A personal budget is an account of your income and expenses for a given period of time, preferably a month. A budget will show you how much income you expect to have in the month and what expenses you expect to incur. Creating a budget may not sound fancy to many people because they think it is a restrictive tool, but it helps one to keep their financial house in order.

One very important thing is that you need to be truthful about your income and your expenditure. You should not deliberately overestimate or underestimate figures. Try to be as accurate as possible in stating your figures, so that even if the actual may differ from the estimated, it will not do so by much. Here are the steps to follow in creating a personal budget:

1. Gather Your Financial Information

You need to be aware of all your possible income sources. You need to have all your financial information at hand, this includes your income sources, your bank statements if available, credit card bills, receipts from the last three months, and your recurring expenses. The more financial information you can gather the better. Bring to the table anything that you think has to do with your finances. This is your starting point in creating your budget.

2. Calculate Your Income

You must have an idea of how much income you expect to receive every month. You probably know where your money comes from every month, and how much it adds up to. Make sure you account for all your income sources. Many people tend to have other sources of income that they consider separate and do not include in their budgeting process. Avoid this. Your income may be variable—you may not be sure of how much it will be in the month. In this case, you should take into account the income from your lowest earning month and use it for the budget.

3. List Your Monthly Expenses

You must be able to come up with a list of all the expenses that you expect to incur in that particular month. You can make use of your credit card statements, bank statements, and receipts to track your spending. Your expenses may include categories like groceries, self-care, savings, and travel.

4. Define Your Fixed and Variable Expenses

Fixed expenses are those expenses for which you pay the same amount every month. These are pretty easy to budget for because they are exact. Such expenses as rentals and internet services and fixed debt repayments. Variable expenses differ from month to month and have to work with an estimate when preparing a budget. These are such expenses as utility bills. The charge will directly depend on usage. Define these expenses for yourself and note them down as accurately as possible.

5. Establish Your Income and Expenditure Totals

After having established your income and your expenses, you need to come up with totals. If your income is higher than your expenses, congratulations on starting on such a good note. If your expenses are higher than your income, then you need to consider reviewing your spending habits.

6. Adjust Your Expenses

If you are operating on a deficit budget, where your expenses are higher than the income, find areas where you can cut back on variable expenses. These may include, as mentioned earlier, taking out packed lunches and eating out less. Depending on how much of a deficit you have, trimming your variable expenses only may not be enough to balance the budget or bring it to a surplus. You may have to cut back even on the fixed costs or find alternative ways to increase your income to balance things out.

The 50-30-20 Budget Rule

The 50-30-20 budget rule is a simple plan that helps people achieve their financial goals (Whiteside, 2020). The rule states that 50% of your disposable income should be directed towards your needs and obligations. These are the necessities that you cannot do without and must have at all costs. You absolutely must pay for them and they are key to your survival. These include groceries, health care, and utilities. You should teach yourself that half of your income is all that you need to survive. If your needs exceed 50% of your after-tax income, you should cut down.

Out of your monthly income, 30% should be directed towards your wants. Wants are those things you can do without but may want to have if you can afford them. They are not essential but are optional. These include movie tickets, game tickets, and gym subscriptions. You should ensure they do not exceed 30% of your remaining income after your needs have been covered. So basically, wants are those extras that you can have to make your life more enjoyable and entertaining, but you can do without. The remaining 20% should be directed towards savings, investment, and debt repayment. From this money, you can add to your emergency fund that we discussed earlier.

You will realize that by teaching yourself to conform to the 50-30-20 budget rule for all of your income, you will be able to better manage your finances. At the end of the day, your needs and wants are catered for, while you have a surplus for investment. The key to wealth creation lies in having a surplus. This rule will help you to achieve that. Therefore, you need to be able to identify your needs as well as your wants. They should be clearly defined to make it easier for you to allocate money to them without encroaching into the allocation for savings. This rule helps you to manage your money and to save for retirement or emergencies.

What Does a Budget Look Like?

There is a lot that could go wrong in your financial life if you operate without a personal budget. You will use your money aimlessly without thinking about the consequences. By constantly visiting your budget, you keep reminding yourself of what you planned for and keep yourself on course. This section will answer the question of what a budget looks like. It gives you a format you can follow in coming up with your own budget. You can of course modify it and include other items that are specific to you.

Table 1: Example of a budget.

INCOME			
Income	Budget	Actual	Difference
Salary	$100.00	$90.00	-$10.00
Interest	$5.00	$6.00	$1.00
Miscellaneous	$5.00	$8.00	$3.00
Others	$11.00	$9.00	-$2.00
TOTAL	**$121.00**	**$113.00**	**-$8.00**

EXPENDITURE			
Expenditure	**Budget**	**Actual**	**Difference**
Groceries	$10.00	$12.00	$2.00
Rentals	$8.00	$8.00	-
Internet and Telephone	$3.00	$4.00	$1.00
Gym Subscription	$5.00	$5.00	-
Class Trip	$20.00	$30.00	$10.00
Lunch	$5.00	$8.00	$3.00
TOTAL	**$51.00**	**$67.00**	**$16.00**

SUMMARY			
Income	$121.00	$113.00	
Expenditure	$51.00	$67.00	
Balance	$70.00	$46.00	

The example budget given above is an example of a surplus budget. You have seen that the budget had a surplus after expenses had been deducted, and so did the actual. The individual had an actual surplus of $2,603. This is approximately 34% of the budget. Following the 50-30-20 rule, you will realize that this individual had more to save and invest than expected. For a balanced budget, the balance would have been zero, because the expenditure would be equal to the income. If the expenses had been more than the income, then there would be a negative balance on the budget which is an indication of overspending.

This template has given you an idea of how you can draft your budget. Perhaps now you can get down to drafting your own budget. If by the time you are done your budget looks anything like the above template, you've started at a good place. If you have a deficit, or you have balanced it out, you need to cut back on your expenditure. As I alluded to earlier, I recommend that one always operate on a surplus budget, because it has room for growth.

Budgeting Tips

To close off the topic of budgeting, here are a few tips that will help you to enhance your financial life.

Make Use of Cash When Spending

The idea behind this tip is that making use of cash when spending is a good way to keep your spending in check. Have you realized that when you make purchases using debit or credit cards, it does not feel like you have spent anything at all? That is why you may overspend and not even realize it. Make it a point for yourself that, whenever you spend money, you have to do it using cash. The fact that you are fishing money out of your pocket to pay for something rings a bell in you whenever you exceed your spending expectation.

Automate Your Saving

Saving is a difficult thing to do. Sometimes you may only remember that you need to save after you have spent your money. To help the situation, you can automate transfers into your savings account from your checking account. You will not have to worry about setting aside cash for savings because before you even handle the money, the job has already been done. You can even separate your savings accounts. For example, you can have the retirement plan and the emergency fund both automated and receiving funds according to your allocation. Try this, and you will thank me later.

Establish Your Saving Goals

Saving is easy if you can establish why you are saving. Saving up for a specific reason is motivation in itself. For example, you can have a car fund, holiday fund, and retirement fund. You can then save money for these reasons, allocating it accordingly. Your saving should therefore not just be saving, but you need to define what you are saving for. It helps.

Save Before Making Big Purchases

Whenever you intend to make big purchases, save up for it. Big purchases should not come out of one month's budget. This would upset the budget and give you a really big deficit. Set aside money for the purchase and ensure your budget can still breathe. Do this for as long as it takes until you have saved up enough. It helps you to grow without crippling yourself with debt.

Conform to Your Budget

Budgeting is like dieting. It requires strict conformity to set guidelines, otherwise, the cause of budgeting is distorted. When you budget, make it a point to adhere to what you laid down in the budget. Being a strict follower of your budget helps you to manage your money better. In many cases, people start with good intentions, but as time goes by, they drift away from their plans and lose focus. Do not be one of them. Focus on bringing your budget to life and you will be able to create wealth from a very young age.

I hope that by now, you have a full understanding of what budgeting is and the importance of having a budget. The book has so far discussed various types of budgets and has provided information on a typical draft of a budget. This information put to good use will help you as a starting point to your journey of wealth creation starting from now.

Chapter 2:

Investment

We discussed saving in detail at the beginning of this book, and that it is important to save before spending. The main focus of this book is to teach young people how to create wealth for themselves and learn to manage their finances from a very young age. This chapter discusses the most important aspect of wealth creation and accumulation—investment.

Investment is the allocation of money in the hope of some benefit or returns in the future. It entails owning an asset, physical or financial, with the expectation of generating income from the investment over time. Some assets appreciate over time. In investment, you have to outlay an asset today, and the payoff in the future should be greater than what was originally put in. In financial terms, an investment is an asset acquired with the intention of allowing it to grow in value over time.

Any action taken today with the hope of benefit in the future can be considered an investment. This can involve time, money, and effort. There is always a certain level of risk involved. You can either win or lose. Investment is like sowing. You may or may not reap. Many people have, however, benefited from investment. These people are those that managed to be risk-takers and to invest in the face of uncertainty. After saving, instead of keeping the money tied in a savings account, you can choose to carefully invest. Investment is the key to wealth creation. When you invest, returns from your investment grow your wealth.

Investment in financial assets can include the purchase of bonds, stocks, and real estate property. These are expected to generate a certain level of income over time. This may, or may not, be the case at the end of the day, but not investing is not an option either. You need to be able to draw a line between investing and not investing. Saving is the accumulation of money without any risk involved. Investing, on the other hand, bears a lot of risks, and the investor risks making a loss from the investment.

Of importance, you should note that you cannot invest unless you have saved. Saving starts first—and then you can invest. Not vice versa. You do not invest to save but you save to invest. If you have hopes to venture into investment someday, then start saving immediately to make it possible. If you have been saving for a while now, you may start considering your investment options.

Important Terms

We will start the chapter by defining some terms pertaining to investment that you need to comprehend to make the chapter easier to understand.

Interest

Interest is the amount of money a lender or investor receives for lending or investing money. It is usually expressed as a percentage of the initial investment. For example, you could earn 10% monthly interest on your investment of $300, which means your investment increases by $30 every month. Interest can also be compounded depending on how you invest. Growing your wealth, therefore, depends on earning interest in your investments.

Figure 2: You can earn interest from your investments.

Investment Horizon

This is the total length of time that an investor intends to hold an asset or portfolio. It is important to have a clearly set out horizon because it determines the amount of time you will hold your investments to compensate for the risks involved in investing. You should also understand that the longer the horizon, the more money—and vice versa.

Initial Outlay

In the case of investment, this refers to the initial amount you need to invest to get yourself started. This is the total outflow of cash you invest in different assets to make up a portfolio. The idea is that at the end of the horizon for a certain asset, the total consolidated cash flows should have grown significantly as compared to the initial outlay. If your yield is less than the initial outlay, needless to say, you have made a loss.

The Stock Market

The stock market is the place where the shares of public listed companies are traded. You can buy and sell shares on the stock market to make a profit. The dealership lies in buying stocks and reselling them at a higher price. One has to carefully watch the market trends so that they can sell their stocks at a time they consider the yield to be the highest it can ever be. A stock can also be sold if there is a prediction of its value declining. You would then want to sell it as quickly as possible to avoid making a loss.

Why Is It Important to Invest?

Investment is vital if you have the intention of creating wealth for yourself. Just as you work hard for your money, your money should also work hard for you. Do not keep it idle; put it to work. Investing allows you to generate an extra income stream as well as grow your wealth. Depending on how much ground you want to gain in wealth creation while you are still young, you can decide on whether you want to invest your money or not.

Save for Retirement

Have you realized that those people who do not invest have longer working lives? Retirement is never an option for them because they will not have other means of survival should they do so. Ideally, everyone would want to reach a certain age and retire comfortably, but the key to such financial stability is the investment made today. As young as you are, you must always remind yourself that there will come a time when you will not be able to work anymore. You can have your retirement savings invested in stocks, mutual funds, or bonds. Do not let money lie idle in savings accounts— invest it, create returns, and build wealth for yourself. It is worth the risk.

Grow Your Money

One can indeed grow their money into unbelievable sums. After investing, you will begin to get returns in the long run. The wealth you dream of is the money that you have today given the opportunity to grow. It is as simple as that. Make it a point from a young age to grow your wealth by a certain percentage every year. Give yourself investment return targets. The target will keep you looking for viable investment opportunities and such engagement will see you realizing more income than you thought you could.

Beat Inflation

If you leave your money lying idle in your savings or checking accounts, it will decline in purchasing power, and its value will be eroded by inflation. Inflation is the continuous increase in prices of goods and services which in turn diminishes the purchasing power of money. Reported inflation can be low, but the cost of living increases over time at a rate much faster than is reported. The interest paid to you if you choose to keep your funds in your savings account is way less than the return you could make if you choose to invest. This difference could be all you need to beat inflation.

Aspects Of Investment to Bear In Mind

Investment is not a simple thing as it may appear to most of us, especially at a young age. There are some important facts explained here that you need to understand before you venture into investment. Try by all means to ensure that your investment is:

1. Long Term

You must understand that long-term investments can grow very big over time. You should be patient enough to wait as your investment grows. Long-term investment lasts for anything above ten years. Some investments can be scheduled in such a way that the investor knows how much it will grow to at the end of the time period. This is especially possible if the economic environment is stable enough to allow constant growth of your investment.

Consider an investment as a method of putting money away in something that grows and will make you a wealthier person over time. Don't expect investments to yield quickly, because they may not. Giving it time is the best way to figure your investment out and to allow it time to mature and outlive the fluctuations in the market. For example, if you invest $300 every month with compound interest of 10%, you will get more than a million and a half in 40 years. You can even build and grow a business that grows your money faster so you will not have to wait for forty years.

2. Secure

We cannot say that you will at any time make a secure investment. Nothing is secure, but you need to study your investment and have as much knowledge about it as possible. Do not invest your money in a property or stocks if you do not know what you are doing. If you must buy a stock, do so in a solid company to ensure that your investment is as secure as possible. Of course, nothing can be 100% secure, but at least you can increase security by having as much knowledge about your investment as possible.

3. Supervised and Not Delegated

Many people are tempted to delegate their money to someone else who will invest it on their behalf. This is risky. Do not have your money invested in assets that you do not have control over. When you invest, you of course cannot control the market, but you can control your positions, and even de-invest if you want to. You must therefore be "hands-on" in the supervision of your investment, even if it has been done on your behalf. Do not give anyone control of your money without an awareness of what is going on with it. It is alright to get advice on your investment option—but you should be the one to call the shots.

Types of Investment

Having discussed the importance of investment, the next question you may have is how to invest—and in what assets. Let us discuss the categories of investment that can be implemented by an individual.

Ownership Investment

This is when an individual purchases and owns an asset. These could be stocks, bullion, and real estate. Investment into a business is also a type of ownership investment. You can own an asset, a company, or part of it.

Stocks are shares of ownership in a company. This means that you invest in a certain percentage of the company's value and ultimately own it. Stocks can also be called equities. They allow you to share in the profits of the company according to your percentage of ownership. You also share in the losses of the company, and if the value of the company depreciates, so does the value of your stock. Real estate is another form of ownership investment. This includes houses, apartments, and other buildings or land that you acquire to rent or to resell. The idea to resell at a later date is generally embedded in the idea that real estate assets appreciate in value over time. Other assets that can be owned include precious objects like metals, art, and collectibles.

Lending Investments

Lending money is a form of investment. The risks are lower for many investments, and the rewards are modest. These include government bonds, which will pay out a higher amount than the initial outlay at a later date. Remember also that when you deposit money with a bank, you are lending them your money so that they can use it and give it back to you when you need it. They will pay back with interest, of course. The risk in this type of investment is quite low, and so are the returns. The higher the risk involved, the higher the payout.

Cash and Cash Equivalents

Cash equivalents refer to those investments that are as good as cash. This can even be as simple as a savings account or a money market fund. In general, a certain percentage of your portfolio will consist of cash. Investing in these is another type of investment that can equally yield revenue for you if managed well. To spread risk, you may consider having different types of investments in your portfolio to boost security.

Investing Tips for Beginners

There are some important investment tips that one should adhere to in order to grow their wealth. Many young people are lured into investment and invest with just the excitement to put their money to work. They then find their money sinking or experiencing great financial risk. It is therefore important to enter into an investment with a little bit of knowledge that prepares you for what to expect and how to act accordingly. Here are some investing tips that you should master before you invest.

Understand Why You Are Investing

Wealth creation is the bigger picture you should ever lose sight of. If you do not have an understanding of why you are investing, you may invest just out of excitement and lose sight of the bigger picture. Have long-term goals for your investment, so that you settle down and map your investment plan. Have a target for each investment and act accordingly to ensure you get there. Make sure the goals are attainable so that they do not end up demotivating you.

Pay Off Debt

Pay off your debts as much as you can before you start investing. High-interest debt like credit cards will cripple your finances. Being debt-free before you invest will help you to grow because the income from the investment is accumulated. When you are in debt, you have to make interest payments, and the income from an investment may be swallowed up in these payments.

Have an Emergency Fund

The idea about having an emergency fund is not just setting aside money that will help you when you encounter an emergency. I want you to understand that prior to investment, you should secure yourself financially as much as possible. Before you invest, take time to set aside cash that can cover your monthly expenses for a reasonable time frame, say three to nine months. This secures your long-term investments because you will not be forced to liquidate them to cover emergencies.

Understand Your Monthly Expenses

Knowing your expenses helps you to determine how much you can start with in investing. The expenses section of your budget may fluctuate, but it should so around a certain orbit. You should be able to limit the fluctuations to a certain percentage. This is an indication that you will have mastered the art of controlling your expenses in such a way that they can be factored into a yearly budget with close to accurate figures. Know what you spend your money on every month. Understanding your expenses will also help you to see where you need to cut back so that any extra money can be directed towards investment.

Invest In Something You Understand

There are a whole lot of options for your investment. These options are lucrative in varying ways. Investment specialists may lure you into investing in funds that "they" think are doing great, while you personally do not have any knowledge of whether or not it is so. One important thing is to always invest in something you understand. Do not just follow the crowd. Take time to understand what you are investing in and decide for yourself if you want to invest. Of course, a little expert advice may be of help, but you need to have some knowledge of your own, too.

Understanding investment options will also help you not to jump onto investment trends. The norm about these trends is that the asset being invested in may seem lucrative for some time, but eventually, it fades away. Read around to understand investments and what choices offer the best stability before you start. Go through personal investment books to learn—and continue to learn throughout your investment journey. Investment may not look complicated on the outlook, but there is a lot of information around it that you need to digest before you can make great investment choices.

Learn to Read and Understand a Prospectus

Having discussed the importance of understanding your investment, it is also important for you to understand the prospectus of your potential investment. A prospectus is the bigger picture of your investment. It is an overview of what you are investing in provided to the public by the holders of the asset. Being able to comprehend a prospectus helps the investor to make informed investment decisions concerning the asset they want to invest in. The prospectus helps you to understand what to expect. This could be the fees, the returns, and a general understanding of the company you are investing in.

Diversify

You want to reap as much as possible from your investments, and therefore it is wise for you to diversify your portfolio. Depending on your investment horizon, you must choose what to include in your portfolio. It is said that you should not have your eggs in one basket. Investing in one asset type is risky because if the asset value drops, so does your overall financial status. Investing in a wide array of assets helps to keep you afloat because, even if some assets are failing, others may be doing well.

Reinvest Capital Gains

As a young person, spending out of your first capital gains may be tempting. The best way to move forward, however, is to reinvest any dividends and capital gains automatically. Only after having grown your investment in such a way that the capital gains are sizable should you start considering using some money from the investment. In most cases, because you are still young, you may not have very much to invest in, and as a result, the capital gains are quite low. You can grow your portfolio by continued reinvestment over a certain period of time. That is how wealth is gradually created.

Occasionally Rebalance Your Portfolio

There is no stipulation about how often you should balance your portfolio. Yearly rebalancing may, however, be ideal. By rebalancing, you are restructuring or repositioning your investment according to your ratio. For example, you may have initially chosen to have 70% in stocks and 30% on bonds. Fluctuations and changes in the market may upset the balance of your portfolio and you will need to rebalance it occasionally.

Having mastered these and other investment tips, you are good to go. Understand the basic terminology in investment and have an appreciation of how to value an investment before getting into it. Investment professionals may try to talk you into investments that offer them a high commission, but do not pay you much. Research each investment and invest knowingly. You must also know how to study the market trends and the world economy. It helps you to be a financially sharp individual.

How to Start Investing With Little Money

Earlier in this book, I explained that you cannot invest unless you have saved up some money and that you do not have to wait until you have amassed a large sum of money to start investing; the reason we talk of large and small investments is that people invest differently according to their capacity. With the advent of online investment and other innovations, it has now become possible to invest little money. Here are a few ideas on how you can go about investing small amounts of money.

Figure 3: Start investing little money and grow it.

Put Your Money In Initial-Investment Mutual Funds

Mutual funds are investment securities that allow you to invest in stocks and bonds in a single transaction. This makes them perfect for new investors. Mutual funds, however, have minimums for the investment an individual can make. Being a first-time investor, these minimums may be out of your reach. Some mutual fund companies may, however, agree to review the minimums if you can make automatic monthly investments that will add up to their initially stipulated minimum amount.

Invest Little Money Into the Stock Market

The major barrier to entry into the stock market is the cost associated with an investment. The times have changed though, and the internet has enabled investors to start with very little money. You can even play around in the stock market with little money so that you can familiarize yourself with the system. This is a good way to learn about investment without putting much money at risk. In the conventional way of investment in the stock market, the stockbrokers would charge a commission of several dollars for every investment you would make. The current investment system through the internet has opened a lot of new doors for potential investors who can invest from as little as $1 with no trade commissions. It is wise to start in this way.

The Cookie Jar Approach

As explained in the opening of this chapter, to invest you need to save up money first. Do not see this as an obstacle. It is really easy to save up a little money to start yourself off. Find ways to make saving easier for you. Try saving a certain amount per week, and putting it into an envelope, a shoebox, or the legendary cookie jar. It may sound ineffective, but it is a necessary first step to start you off on saving. The savings account is the electronic alternative to the cookie jar.

Enroll In a Retirement Plan

You can start by investing in your employer-sponsored plan that you can afford. You can invest as little as 2% of your salary and you will not even notice it. Even if you are on a tight budget, this is something you can do. You can increase the contribution gradually as your salary increases or as your budget loosens up. It is a good way to start saving even with very little monthly income.

Start an Online Business

Starting an online business is one of the easiest ways to make money for yourself. This is a business that is run on the internet. It is also called e-business. Starting an online business is definitely an exciting venture. It, however, is not as easy as it might seem. One needs to be organized and determined to make it work. The online business world is pretty congested and you need to put in the effort to set yourself apart from the rest. An online business can be anything from selling goods online, coaching and consulting, digital marketing service, freelancing, and virtual assistant work. You can do this from the comfort of your home, and therefore very little capital is needed. This is an ideal business type for young people, who are highly computer literate and want to start making money at a young age.

Figure 4: Online business is viable.

What Assets to Invest in

With enough help and expertise, you can decide which assets you want to invest in. It is important, however, for you to have an appreciation of what kind of assets you could possibly put your money into.

Stocks

This is a term used to describe the ownership certificates of a company. A share is therefore the stock certificate of a particular company. If you hold shares in a company, you become a shareholder. A shareholder is a part-owner of the company and they benefit from the profits made by the company according to the ownership ratio.

Real Estate

This refers to property consisting of land and buildings. It sometimes refers to land and the improvements attached to the land. These include water, minerals, buildings, and even fences. Real estate offers a profit because it increases in value. The profit can always be realized by selling the asset or renting it out for a period of time enough to cover the initial outlay.

Bonds

These are known as fixed income instruments. They are used by the government or companies to raise money by borrowing from investors. The investor buys the bond at an amount lower than the payout on the day of liquidation. The value of bonds can change over time. The higher the chance of being paid back on time, the lower the interest rates and vice versa.

This chapter has discussed in detail the things you need to understand about investment as a young person. By now you are aware that investment is the best you can do for yourself if you dream of creating wealth. Do not be scared of investment. Remember that the higher the risks, the greater the return. It is time for you to put your money together and start yourself off on the journey of creating financial liberty for yourself through investment.

You can never get to know everything involved in investment before you start; this chapter has given you information on the basics of investment and the important facts you need to familiarize yourself with. The rest of the knowledge will be acquired in the process. You become more and more experienced in investment by the day. Investment is not only for the old—dare to be different and start now. The earlier, the better!

Chapter 3:

How Money Works

We have so far discussed how to manage money and how to create wealth through saving and investment. The good thing about this is that it makes you a better person financially and helps you to manage your money well. However, one also needs to understand what money is, how it is created, the facts surrounding it, and what affects its value over time. Money, in any form, can lose or appreciate in value over time. A sound understanding of how money works is therefore key in enhancing a person's financial wisdom.

The first question that this chapter will answer is the question about what money is. This question is hardly ever asked because we all think we know what money is, but by answering it, you will gain an understanding of the bigger picture of the money system. This understanding will help you to easily understand cycles, trends, and basic information about money according to your type of economy.

You need to understand how money works. You need to understand the generation of money and that it is the result of selling value to the market. For example, this book you are reading is made up of valuable pieces of information that you paid for. If the market is not paying for your product then the product has no market value. You may think that a product is of a certain value but if the market does not think so, then the market value is zero. Personal value and market value are two different things. You need to provide value to the market. That is how money is generated.

Employees earn money because they are selling value to the employer—although they may do so without even knowing. An employer may have done all the work by himself before he hired an employee. Now the employee gets to do the employer's tasks and gets paid for them. They are freeing up time for the employer to sell more value to the market than the salary they are paying the employee. Unfortunately, some employees may not understand why they are getting paid or how much value they are adding to the organization. For the employee to earn more, they must make themselves irreplaceable.

What Is Money?

Money is a recognized and centralized medium of exchange that is generally accepted in an economy. It is used to facilitate transactional trade for goods and services. Money operates in the form of a commodity, having some physical properties that are adopted by participants in the market as a medium of exchange. Money can take many forms. It can be in the form of electronic cryptocurrencies, money substitutes, or officially issued legal tender.

Figure 5: Money

Commonly, money is referred to as currency, and each government has an acceptable money system of its own. There has also been the advent of cryptocurrencies that are now being widely used to facilitate international trade. Money operates based on its general acceptance in an economy or international trade. The value of money is not derived from the material used to produce the money, but from the face value printed on it is generally accepted as the true value in exchange. You will note that the same material may be used to produce different notes and coins, but the difference is in the features and the value assigned to it.

According to Bagus (2020), the value of money is derived from the willingness to agree to the value displayed. Having understood this, we can then talk of the primary function of money: a medium of exchange that is generally recognized and that people and economies intend to hold and accept as payment for both current and future transactions. Money was first introduced to replace bartering, which was the exchange of goods and services for other goods and services. For example, someone would exchange a cow for a horse. Money came in to provide a centralized system of exchange because it helped overcome double coincidence of wants.

Double coincidence of wants is a problem that was prominent in the barter economy, where to trade, each party was required to have something that the other party wanted. If the case was not so, then no trade would take place. The use of money addressed this problem because as long as both parties use and accept the currency agreed upon, then trade can always take place. There are, however, certain qualities and features that money should possess for it to be acceptable and useful. It should be:

1. Durable

The physical character of money is that it should be durable enough to be reused many times and to retain its usefulness for future transactions. A perishable medium of exchange will not be useful enough for future exchanges, because it will have depreciated in value. Whether used today, tomorrow, or any other day, money should retain its face value. Imagine if a note worth $10 today was of a lesser value tomorrow. That would mean it cannot be widely accepted as money because the value attached to it is not universal.

2. Portable

Money should be divisible into small amounts. The general idea about the portability of money is that it should be easy to carry around or be transported. It can be difficult to deal with an immovable good or one that is indivisible and non-portable. This could present high transaction costs either in transporting large quantities of the good or in transferring the ownership of the good. The portability of money makes it easy to make transactions between individuals, groups, or companies.

3. Recognizable

The authenticity and value of the good being widely accepted as money should be readily ascertainable so that the terms of an exchange can be quantified and accepted. You should be able to recognize a certain unit of currency without having to think. The use of non-recognizable goods as money creates the problems of non-acceptability because either party could value the good differently and one party may be reluctant in accepting the value purported by the other.

4. Stable

The value placed on a good that is widely accepted as money should be stable or should appreciate over time.

A good whose value is constantly going up or down cannot be universally accepted as money because, at any point in time, the value may change. It will be less ideal for players in the market to hold the currency. Fraudulent dealings will also be on the increase if one of the exchange parties is not aware of the current value of the money.

You probably have now gained an understanding of how money came to be, and what qualities it should possess for it to be generally accepted as money. We will now take a look at the functions of money, other than as a medium of exchange.

Functions of Money

From its use as a medium of exchange, we shall discuss the secondary functions of money. Understanding these will help you to make your money function better for you.

Unit of Account

Money can be used to keep track of the gain or loss made from multiple transactions and to compare the value of certain combinations of goods and services mathematically (Ingham, 2004). This function of money derives from its use as a medium of exchange for buying and selling and from its use in assigning prices to goods and services. We can therefore say money is the language in which the value of business is spoken. Through the use of money, we can talk of profit and loss, budgeting, and the valuation of a company or an individual's net worth.

Store of Value

Money functions as a way to store value from current trade for use in the future. If one holds money, they hold value that can work for them whenever they call on it. This is the reason why we talk about saving money. Ideally, you will be accumulating value for future use, in the form of currency and not other physical assets. Individuals can therefore trade goods and services that are not durable, or widely acceptable for money, which they can store and use later because of its wide acceptance.

Standard of Deferred Payment

This is a function of money where it is a widely accepted way to value a debt. It allows goods and services to be acquired now and paid for later. Deferring payments means payments are completely or partially postponed for financial reasons. These help in a lot of ways, for example, helping a student facing financial hardships to complete their education and pay later.

Types of Money

Historically, gold was used as a form of money. Farmers would exchange their produce at the marketplace in exchange for gold. You should understand that on its own, money is worthless. The trust that people bestow upon it is what gives money value. For other types of money, such as commodity money, there is an element of the store of value.

Commodity Money

It is difficult to ascertain the origin of money, although history has it that commodities like gold were once accepted as a form of money. The origins of money date back to the Lydian merchants who produced a coin from gold mixed with silver and made it a standardized unit of value (Boyce, 2021). It helped traders to convert money and trade internationally.

Commodity money has a store of value, unlike other forms of money. It is physical, and even if nations no longer use the commodity, it still retains its value. A commodity is a real thing, and the value of commodity money depends on what builds people's trust in it. You can see and touch commodity money. This is what sets it apart from other types of money which cannot be touched or seen but depend on the trust of its value.

Commodity money may have other uses besides it being used as a medium of exchange. For example, items like gold, silver, and tobacco have uses that they can be put to besides being used as money. So, if one trader was to reject a commodity as a form of money, it would be acceptable elsewhere. Economically, we can therefore say commodity money has intrinsic value. Therefore, put simply, commodity money can be put to many other uses.

Commodity money was prominent in the past because it was a good store of value. It was widely accepted and could be trusted. Back then, people trusted the gold coin stamped with the royal seal just as much as we trust government-backed money today. Commodities such as salt and tobacco were mainly used as commodity money because they were high in demand and even if one part did not want it, it could be traded with a third party.

Fiat Money

Fiat money, described in easy terms, are pieces of paper issued with solemnity and authority that would match pure gold or silver. On those pieces of paper, officials would write their names and put their seals. As a result, fiat money only has value because of people's trust in it. The government declares it as legal tender, and because of that, it becomes widely accepted. This is the most common form of money in use today.

Fiat money has no intrinsic value. It cannot be used for purposes other than that of being a medium of exchange. With the use of fiat money, inflation is likely to occur because there is no limit on its supply. Commodities can be limited, but not fiat money. There is only so much gold or silver in the world, but fiat money has no limit to it. Fiat money commonly used today comes in the form of banknotes and coins—this is when we get to talk of currencies, for example, the Euro, Dollar, or Pound. Notes that were used in exchange for gold and silver can, however, not be listed as fiat money because they are backed by a commodity with intrinsic value.

This type of money is more stable than other forms of money. The supply is steadily controlled by the central bank. The use of fiat money gives the government a lot of control over the money supply. There is no limit, however, to how much the government can print and this sometimes results in inflation. For example, in politically hyped times, the government may want to campaign by giving out free stuff to the public. There may be no other way to fund this besides printing new money. At the end of the day, the market becomes flooded, and inflation results.

This has, however, been curbed by the operation of central banks that have independence from the government. These banks are self-funded and have a set mandate to follow. They have to ensure economic stability and hold inflation as low as is possible.

Commercial Bank Money

Commercial bank money refers to debt that is created through the fractional reserve system (Zeder, 2016). The way the system works is that out of a deposit of $100, the bank holds on to $10 to cater to depositors' short-term withdrawals, and loans out the other $90. This is called the money multiplier effect. This is the system used by commercial banks today, where they lend out part of what they receive in order to create money.

Commercial bank money is debt created by banks through the use of customer's fiat money. The bank, therefore, has money going around—and in—creating more money through the interest paid by borrowers on their borrowed funds.

How to Make Money Work For You

The idea of saving money may end up not being a good one if inflation is high and your money is losing its value as it lies idle in your savings account. Your money needs to be growing at a higher rate than that of inflation for it not to lose value. As a result, it is very important to find ways to make your money work for you without incurring a significant loss from trying to save money. The idea about saving and investment is that your money should grow at a rate higher than inflation. If it doesn't, it is decreasing in value every day and it will have depreciated by a significant percentage at the end of the year.

You should get the most out of your money while you still can. This can involve sorting out your debts and making higher-risk investments. Here are some tips on how you can make your money work for you.

Budget

You must always be able to create a workable budget that stops you from wasting your money. You learned earlier how to create a workable budget and you must teach yourself to adhere to it. Adjustments should be made only when absolutely necessary. The first draft of your budget is usually the most effective and the most correct reflection of your financial aspirations.

Pay Off Debts

Good savings and investments have the advantage of outperforming the high rates from loans, mortgages, and credit cards. The better you save and invest, the higher your ability to offset the debt. Once you have offset the debt, you will be able to reinvest the returns from investing and save more. That is healthy financial growth. In order for you to clear debt, you first all need to determine how much you owe. You must know the total amount that you owe, then you can devise a good strategy to get rid of it. You should decide how you are going to pay off your debt (Sethi,

2019). You can decide what installment to pay on each debt in order to free yourself as quickly as possible.

Invest In Your Education

One good way of making use of your money is to get yourself a good education. Investing in your education increases your market value and helps you to secure a better job and a better salary. Instead of having the money lie low, pay for your fees and learn whatever you are passionate about. A good education is better capital than money.

Start Your Own Business

Most of us have business ideas that may never have come to fruition by the time we die. Starting your own business is a perfect idea if you have an idea or a certain skill. One way to do this would be to leave your job and start out on your own in the same line of business. The easiest business to start is that of your employer because you have all the knowledge it takes to get it to work.

Rent Assets Out

Sometimes you may have your money lodged in valuable assets that you could make money out of if only you could rent them out. Instead of just holding on to the value of the asset and depending on the market for the assets' appreciation on value, rent them out. Renting out the things you have can be a good way to make money for yourself.

These are just a few tips on how you can get money to work for you. It is a good way to create more value and to make sure you enjoy the benefits of your investment and savings. As much as you may want to create wealth to enjoy much later in life, you do not know whether or not you will outlive the horizon of your investment. Sneak out one or two benefits from your money while you still can. It is your money.

While we may discuss how to make money work for you, there is that one person who has no money to put to work. This part will discuss how to create money out of nothing. It is possible to start earning money without investing any. For many young people, the following tips are a good place to start. You can boost your earnings, invest, and save out of the money you make from no investment. Here's how.

Request a Pay Raise

This may seem a funny way of raising money to start, but it is worth trying. Sometimes we live on such tight budgets that it is difficult to have anything left for ourselves. Saving or investing is something not worth mentioning in such a scenario. If you do not see any other way to raise money for yourself, request a pay raise. If you are successful, get by the way you have always done and save or invest the raise. It is a good way to start yourself off.

Consulting

Consulting is a good business that requires very little or no capital. If you have something that you are knowledgeable about, or have experience in, you may be able to advise someone and get paid for it. What capital would you need to advise someone? The only important thing is to sell yourself to your potential customer and make a great delivery. That is some easy money to make.

Online Tasks

Online jobs are good ways to make money for yourself. You can get into freelance writing, website reviewing, or data entry. These are good ways to make money with no money from your home. Be on the lookout for ads looking for help and offer it online. You can also create and sell digital products. They include websites, graphics, and software. These can be easily sold through social media, websites, and online marketplaces.

If you think there is nothing you are good at, you can learn everything online through online courses or even for free through Youtube videos. All you need is willpower because all the information is out there—there are no excuses today for not being able to do anything.

Blogging

Blogging is writing, photography, and other media that is self-published online. You can earn a lot of money from advertisements, such as Bing advertisements, sponsored posts, and other sources.

Sell Online

You can sell things that you already have, online products, or handicrafts online. This can be done through platforms like Amazon and eBay which help you to push your products more. Looking to physical markets only for sales may be a daunting task and may require more capital than selling online. Online sales have become a widely accepted way of selling—so go for it.

Chapter 4:

Isolation

While advice, influence, and mentorship play key roles in nurturing a person into a successful individual, most of the influence should come from within you. You are free to dream as big as you want, but sometimes the negative influence of our environment delays or completely halts us. The mind is a powerful tool that has creative abilities. What the mind firmly believes, the body can achieve. One, therefore, has to watch out for influence that brings in negativity and doubt.

Despite being a young person, you have learned to budget your money and to make worthwhile investments. Furthermore, you have acquired an understanding of what money is and how it works. This puts you in just as good a position as adults to start growing yourself financially and to achieve your goals. This chapter will discuss in detail what you need to do to make your own idea successful by enhancing your ability to filter out negative influence.

Many times, we blame the negative filter from our environment as the most common cause of failure. Have you, however, realized that the most influential voice is the one from within? One may want to isolate themselves from the crowds so that they stay focused. They should also isolate themselves from their own negative thoughts, which are more detrimental. This chapter will also detail how you can enhance positive thinking within yourself.

How to Stop Negative People From Influencing You

As is often said, one bad apple can spoil the whole basket. There are people in life who are gifted at sowing negativity and wreaking havoc. The bad attitudes these people possess can infiltrate your mind and cause you to think likewise. Being a young person with an ambition to create wealth, you need to be wary of whoever talks to you concerning that and what information you take in.

Negative people can cause problems for us at an individual level (Morin, 2015). You should have set boundaries. You should be able to identify when these negative individuals overstep into your life in an unwelcome manner. Sometimes, we allow these people to have an influence on our thoughts without knowing it. We tend to believe that their thinking is justified and probably correct. There is nothing right about negativity. You must never be influenced. At the end of the day, your personal power should rule. Here's how you can help yourself escape negativity:

Choose Your Attitude

You cannot tell which attitude is negative if you do not define a positive attitude for yourself. You should have full knowledge of what you consider acceptable so that you can filter out anything negative. You must make a conscious effort to choose your attitude. Tell yourself to stay positive despite the attitudes of the people around you. If you choose to be of a positive attitude, stick to it. Whenever you face challenges, take time to see the positive of them. Have an attitude that defies all odds. Keep telling yourself positive affirmations like, "I can make it," or "It is possible".

Guard Your Time

It is possible to spend two hours dreading an hour's meeting with a negative person. Without knowing it, you have given that person three hours of your time (Morin, 2015). Some people's negativity can influence you even in their absence. You spend so much time thinking about and fearing the negativity when instead you could have been thinking about something positive.

Figure 6: Manage your time well.

Whenever negative thoughts are coming, choose to think about the positive and start positive conversations. Do not allow negativity to take any of your time. Take control of your power by limiting the amount of time you spend thinking about negative things, hating someone, dreading a particular thing, or worrying about unpleasant people.

Seek Positive People

It is a rare and precious ability to be able to look on the bright side in the face of negativity. In order to keep yourself balanced and focused on your goal, you should seek out positive people. Some people are so positively influential that even a little time spent with them is very fruitful. Identify those people in your life, associate with them, and learn from them. Whenever you think that you are not going to make it, go and spend time with a jovial person who will uplift your spirits and give you the desire to try again. There is more to life than what is in the mind of a negative person. Why let them determine your destiny?

Trust Yourself

You need to be confident in your choices and decisions. If you do not trust your own opinion, you find yourself depending upon the opinions of others. You know better what your ambitions and desires are, and you know your abilities. Conviction is a powerful tool that will prompt others to follow you and to trust your opinions. Know what you want and do just that. The moment you let people make vital choices for you, you open yourself up to a whole can of worms. They will eat your dreams up.

Understand Your Strengths and Weaknesses

You are not a perfect person, and you will never be. You have strengths and weaknesses. These strengths are what propel you towards the achievement of goals, and your weaknesses may deter you if you do not know how to deal with them. Acknowledge your weaknesses and be kind to yourself. Avoid situations and people that trigger your weaknesses. Try to be in control of yourself and to make sure you focus more on the positive.

How to Stop Negative Thoughts
From Taking Control

Treatment is pretty straightforward with most external wounds. Treating your thought process is not as easy (Elmer, 2018). It is especially so if the negative thoughts stem from anxiety, depression, and other mental health conditions. You have to put in a lot of effort to avoid negativity.

Shift Your Mindset

To shift the way you think, you are consciously stopping yourself from an established thought pattern. It is like switching gears in your brain so that one you prefer operates. It is quite possible to undo mental programs that you have been operating with. For example, if you have been hard on yourself about having to perform well in most situations, you could find that you put yourself under stressful perfectionism. Be positive with your own thinking and start moving toward your goals with peace of mind.

See the Glass as Half-Full

Figure 7: Half-full or half-empty?

How you answer the question of whether the glass is half-full or half-empty reflects your outlook on life. Positive thinking that is coupled with optimism is key in the journey of wealth creation. A lot of things could go on in your quest to create wealth. Inflation may be eroding your savings, or perhaps your investments may not be yielding as much as you expect them to. Whatever the case, it is helpful to train your mind to see the glass as half-full rather than half-empty. This will guard you from falling back or pulling out because of the challenges you face.

Introduce Positive Self-Talk

Being a positive thinker does not mean you keep yourself busy with positivity and forget the less pleasant situations that life has to offer. Life is a mixed bag—with positives and negatives. Both help you in some way. While focusing on the positive may be ideal, the negative should not be completely ignored because it is what builds us.

Positive thinking begins with positive self-talk. Self-talk is those thoughts that keep running in your head and end up reflecting in your outlook on life. It also involves the affirmations you give to yourself. If your self-talk is more negative than positive, you will probably have a pessimistic outlook on life.

Identify Areas to Change

For you to be a more positive individual, identify areas of your life that you mostly think negatively about and adjust. Try to fall in love with those people or things you normally dread. Whenever a change is possible, do it. Start small, by focusing on one area at a time, until you can conclude that you are a positive person.

Be Open to Humor

It is said that laughter is the best medicine. You should give yourself permission to laugh and smile even in the most trying times. You must be able to find humor in everyday situations. Even in a bad situation, there sure is something to laugh about. This helps you to take things lightly, ward off depression, and be a happier person overall.

Follow a Healthy Lifestyle

Exercising is one way to positively affect mood and reduce stress. Learn stress management techniques and follow healthy diets that give life to your body and mind. Try to exercise for at least 30 minutes every day. You can break this down into smaller fragments of time that you can painlessly stick to. It will make you a better person.

There are several benefits of positivity. These include:

- Lower levels of anxiety
- Better ability to cope during hardships and trying times
- Lower rates of depression
- Increased life span

Given all these, you will realize that it is worthwhile to enhance positivity within yourself. You should try by all means to avoid the effects of negativity on your life. Isolate yourself from negative energy, and eliminate negative thoughts from within yourself. It gives you a better outlook on life and sets your mind for success.

I have realized that in life, friendship and associations have a big role to play in how your life turns out. Friends can either help you to achieve your goals, or they can stop you from achieving them. Friends help us in each and every aspect of life and, therefore, they are an integral part of our lives.

You cannot hang out with people who have no plans, who live life recklessly, and believe that tomorrow will sort itself out. Future success is dependent on how much you take control of your life today. As a young person, you need to get yourself organized right now before you do any damage to yourself that you cannot reverse.

Having long-term plans that require a lot of will usually drive people away from you. This is because these people have no vision about the future—not that there's anything wrong with you. For you to stop thinking about money, you need to make money. When you walk into a restaurant, the first thing you will see on the menu is not the price, but the food. Imagine what an exciting life that would be. Most people do not eat what they want, they eat what they can afford. It is alright if our life starts out in this way, but it is never alright that it remains the same twenty years from now.

An individual is made by the people they spend time around. Most people want to spend money on what they cannot afford. They live artificial lives to keep up with their friends' standards. These peoples' only goal is to save face and not to build wealth for themselves in real terms. If your goal is to create wealth, you cannot afford to hang out with people who do not have this goal. Some of the people may be close to you. These could be parents, siblings, a girlfriend, or a boyfriend. You must keep in touch with them, but do not let them waste your time—stay focused.

What to Look for In an Associate

Joel Osteen said, "You need to associate with people that inspire you, people that challenge you to rise higher, people that make you better. Don't waste your valuable time with people that are not adding to your growth. Your destiny is too important."

Friends have a vital role to play in making our lives. You should not be reckless about your choice of friends (Thrive Global, 2019). It is said that you become like the five people you spend most of your time with. An associate who sees things differently from you and constantly speaks negatively about your dreams is an enemy of progress. A toxic friend is a serious threat to success.

In most cases, as you think, so do you become. If you think you will not make it, it's highly probable that you won't. Now imagine associating with people who think that way. Their negative energy will infiltrate into you. Identify any such people and avoid them, because every time you try to make progress, they will give you a fresh dose of criticism that will pull you down. You need to choose carefully. Your associates should be:

1. Motivational

There is no better motivator than a friend. Friends know you best and they can motivate you to try out things you may not be sure of yourself. Sometimes you face anxiety and may want to give up, but a good friend will hold your hand and drive it in that you can make it. Strong-willed and disciplined people are like a vaccine that helps you to become immune to the temptations that prevent you from staying on course.

Normally, when people cannot control themselves or manage their schedules, they look to people who can manage themselves for encouragement and mentorship. For example, if someone wants to start a weight loss plan, they seek a support group or a personal trainer to help them. Someone more strong-willed than you will help you to grow. You should, therefore, avoid befriending people who are not strong-willed but attach yourself to people who have more willpower in what they do.

2. Challenging

Have you ever realized that a friend may know your strengths and weaknesses better than anyone else? With most people, even our parents or families, we tend to put up faces so that we appear to be behaving the way we are expected to. With a friend, however, you get to loosen up and be your real self. Because they know us that much, our friends should be able to challenge us in the case of life-changing moments. They help to convert our weaknesses into strengths and push us to do better in life.

3. Good Listeners

Associate with people who never get tired of listening to your sob stories. Having a good listener as a friend helps you to do away with stress and depression. You have someone you can vent to. A good friend will take their time to listen and provide you with the opportunity to express your thoughts. Your friends should be part and parcel of your wealth creation quest, not only because they believe in the same things as you do, but because they want the best for you.

4. Good Teachers

Friendship is probably one of the best things that can happen in one's life. Good friends will teach you life lessons. It requires sacrifice, and because someone is willing to sacrifice for you, you find yourself willing to sacrifice for them, too. Friendship teaches us beautiful life lessons that have a positive effect on our goals.

Friends who have the desire to do better in life—and the desire to see their friends doing better, too—are worth keeping. These friends show interest in what you do and will inspire you to do even better. Good associates can inspire you to work harder and to achieve your goals. Because they are interested in your success, they will not let you waiver from your resolutions. Instead, they help you to stick to them and when you finally succeed, they are there to cheer for you. Choosing good friends is necessary if you need to be pushed to do something. If you want to get into business, find someone who has walked the road before to inspire you.

Apart from the qualities you must look for in a friend explained above, one advantage of having good friends is that they improve your health and life. Positive company yields positive results. Friends will always want to see their friends succeed. If they behave otherwise, then they are not good friends—trust me. Your circle of friends should be where you draw most of your inspiration from.

Unless your associations contribute positively to your life, they are not worth having. I always tell people that it is better to have acquaintances than friends because acquaintances do not have much of a bearing on your life. Depending on how close they are to you, your associations can change you. This is why one needs to watch who they associate with.

The Power of Isolation

When you set yourself apart from the crowds, it gives you the ability to focus on what is important in your life. The quest to build wealth and to be a good manager of your finances is not an easy one. The last thing you need is distraction. Isolating yourself from all the noise that distracts you from your focus is very important. Isolation makes you a superpower. Some people have become superpowers and big brands because they made what they stand for so impressionable. People look up to these people because they were able to set themselves apart to achieve their goals.

It is often said that if you do not stand for something, you will fall for anything. As a young person, you should be able to stand for your goals. Be authentic and true to your desires. Some people set goals they deeply want to achieve, but only if they are alone. They cannot share their goals with people because they do not trust themselves enough to be able to filter out negative energy. Authenticity is key to wealth creation. If you decide that you are going to do something, do it. Whether there are people around or not, your goal should remain your goal. Such steadfastness is vital and is better achieved by isolating yourself from negative energy and standing up for who you are.

Isolation gives you consistency and excellence. It allows you enough time to work on your goals and to stick to what you have always done. Consistency in managing your finances helps you to stick to your course of action. You should be consistent in your saving, spending, and investing patterns if you are to achieve your financial goals. It is difficult to remain consistent if you mix yourself up with people who stop you from sticking to your plans. If you want to make it in life, isolate yourself and be consistent with your set game plan. You will ultimately become excellent at managing yourself and your finances.

Of course, isolating yourself does not make you all-powerful or indestructible, but it sure makes failure less probable. You can have the best plans, the necessary knowledge, and expertise, but still fail. Deal with the fact that failure is still possible even when you try as much as possible to isolate yourself. However, it is better to fail after having done your best, than to fail because you were reckless in the way you handled yourself.

If you fail once, you have to look at failure as a lesson that will teach you what not to do or what to do differently the next time. Failure should only exist as a temporary defeat, and never a permanent knockdown. If you never give up, you will never entirely fail. Even if you fail 100 times, you just have to win once.

Chapter 5:

Wrong Purchases

The key to wealth creation is how much control one has over their spending patterns. It is important for an individual who dreams of becoming wealthy someday to manage their spending. Your vision should show in your actions. You cannot be spending like you have made it in life if you are just starting out. The best policy to follow is one that prompts you not to spend unless it is really important.

Having started on the journey of wealth creation, you need to carefully watch yourself so that you do not engage in spending sprees that will leave you grounded. Many people often make the mistake of thinking they have made it in life just after their first investment. They spend like they are already rich and spoil their chances for real success. You wouldn't want to be one of them.

There are many spending mistakes that we keep making. I call them mistakes because they are not supposed to happen. You should not be spending on things that give you nothing more than acceptance by peers. You need to personally improve yourself and invest for a better future. Here are examples of such spending mistakes:

Brand New Car

This is one common mistake we make. It is alright to have the goal of buying a brand new car. It is, however, not a good idea to buy it if it costs more than your income can afford and sustain. The price of that car will decrease by 50% in just one year. If you have enough money, you can afford to be stupid, but if you don't, then you can't. The more methodic and disciplined you are with your money, the more you can afford to be a little stupid sometimes.

Designer Clothes

Sometimes you can get to buy a 100 dollar purse for $1,500. Maybe if you have a very fat bank account and earn $30,000 per month, then you can go ahead and get two of them. Remember, we discussed the fact that you should save a certain percentage of your income every month. So, even after buying the expensive designer clothes, this should never be an excuse for not saving that month. If you save with the intention of spending the money someday, then you are just building liability and not wealth. Spending should be the last thing you do when you get money, otherwise, you cannot get rich.

Reasons Why You Are Overspending

There are many reasons why people spend money, ranging from how they are feeling at a particular moment, to the environments they are in at the time of spending. We need to take a closer look at the reasons why they overspend before trying to address them.

Not Tracking Your Spending

If you do not track your spending, you will never be in charge of your money. You will never know the good feeling of being in total control of your finances, but will rather suffer the guilt and self-blame that causes you to feel like your money owns you. Whether your income is large or small, you need to know what you spend it on. It helps you to know when you are stepping out of the boundaries of what you can afford. Do not be that individual who wakes up having no money and cannot trace where it went.

Retail Therapy

Figure 8: Beware of retail therapy.

This is otherwise known as compulsive spending. Most people spend just because they feel like spending, or because it makes them feel better. Spending—for such people—is a way of getting out of emotional distress because they claim it makes them happier. One sees something and buys it before checking the bank account, or checking their financial goals (Cruze, 2021).

Using Plastic Money More

Everyone loves shopping with someone else's money. You find that you spend more when you are paying with plastic, that is, a debit card or a credit card. The fact that you don't see the money physically will cause you to spend more and still feel okay about it. When you spend with cash, on the other hand, you feel it. The feeling you get when cash leaves your hand into another's will make you not want to go through that unnecessarily—because it hurts.

By spending cash, you are aware of having had cash moments before, and that it is now all gone. That is not so with plastic money. You never physically know the money and you miss out on the trigger that the money is gone. Plastic money makes you feel artificially rich, because in most cases, the money is not even yours.

Peer Pressure

Our actions are influenced by the actions of those around us. When in the presence of a group, we don't act out of reason or common sense, and follow the group's vibe. Being around your peers may prompt you to spend more than planned if they, too, are doing so. You may feel pressured to spend money on something that is considered to be the in-thing because you do not want to feel left out or your peers to feel that you are not fun to be with.

Boredom and Procrastination

Mindless shopping is sometimes a sign that you are avoiding focusing on something. Like when you are supposed to be working on a school project, but do not want to. You may find yourself choosing to do something that causes you to spend money just so you feel better after avoiding work. Shopping feels like a nice way to make yourself feel better when you are bored.

Working Without a Budget

Not having a budget is dangerous to your financial status. It causes you to spend more on something than you should. It is far easier to spend more than reasonable if you do not have a budget. When you don't have a budget, getting into debt is a piece of cake (Johnson, 2016). You will not have even the slightest idea of how much you could be saving. You definitely would have funds to set aside if your spending was planned. Budgeting brings all your financial issues to the table, and forces you to spend according to your standards.

Underestimating Little Expenses

Many times, we tend to take note of the money we pay for big expenses. These could be rentals, or the purchase of a new car. It is, however, those small amounts that collectively weigh down our budgets without us knowing. The dinners, take-out, and gas may be paid for and go almost unnoticed, but if you add them up, the result will shock you. Do not underestimate such small expenses. Take note of them and limit them as much as possible because you may never have a balanced budget unless you do. If you manage to control your spending on such items, you will notice that your wallet will have more breathing space.

Not Having Savings

Many people earn money every month but they do not have savings. Unless someone has been saving up some money, when an emergency happens they will be forced to look to debt for bail-out. Even for small emergencies—like the break-down of a car—one ends up reaching for a credit card or overstepping into money budgeted for other priorities. When at the end of the month the expenses are consolidated, you will realize you have spent more than you can afford.

How to Stop Yourself From Overspending

You have to force yourself to stop spending money unnecessarily. It is a decision you have to make, and engage yourself completely in fighting for your decision. Overspending is an impulsive action. You find you have spent too much but you did not realize it because you were too caught in the moment. Here is how you can put a hold to your spending.

Identify Your Spending Triggers

The first step in trying to control your spending is to identify the emotional and psychological causes. Removing those triggers will help you to remove the temptation to spend. These triggers differ. Your spending may be limited to a certain time of the day or a particular environment. Your spending patterns could also be triggered by peer pressure, mood, and lifestyle. You need to study these and eliminate whatever gives you the urge to spend.

For you to overcome triggers, you can try to do your shopping at that time of the day when you are still energetic; this helps you to think out your purchases before buying and to compare prices. Avoid certain environments that trigger you to spend or make you feel obliged to spend. These environments include shopping malls, craft fairs, or when you are on holiday.

You also need to observe your mood at the time of going shopping. This is because your mood affects your energy levels. If your emotional state is not alright, then you should avoid going shopping because you are most likely to buy things on impulse as long as it makes you feel better. When you are feeling low, go for a walk instead or catch a breath of fresh air to lift up your mood. It helps you to be fair on your money.

Sometimes our spending is triggered when we are around our friends. Being with your peers may trigger you to spend, especially if they also have bad spending habits. Sometimes we may want to spend and go on vacations like our friends do, even if we cannot afford it. It is okay to decline an invitation to lunch, or to stay home if you know it will trigger your spending and you cannot afford it. Always be outspoken enough to let your friends know that you are trying to cut back on your spending. They will help you by not engaging you in events that cause you to spend and, who knows, it may help them too.

Understanding and accepting your lifestyle is also key to cutting back on overspending. You may have been accustomed to a certain lifestyle, but if you are now encountering financial hardships, you should adjust accordingly. You must find out why you feel the urge to spend, because sometimes it may be a result of your upbringing. If you hail from a financially tight background, you may feel the urge to spend in compensation for all the things you were deprived of in your upbringing. Look out for such triggers and control yourself. Remember that the idea of amassing money lies in having it and not spending it recklessly until it accumulates.

Use Cash When You Spend

Do you realize that it is easier and feels more acceptable to use a credit card for your payments than to count out some cash? Using a credit card almost feels like you have not spent at all. Most people forget that money spent through a credit card is still money. This prompts them to overspend because they feel like they have limitless access to cash. The truth is that you cannot afford what you are buying on credit. If you did, why don't you have the money on you?

When you make use of cash, you can track your spending, and you clearly see how funds are declining with each purchase. Because you can do a physical count of the cash you have, you will be able to limit your buying to what you can afford. By using cash, you avoid depending on credit and you stop spending money you do not have. So yes, it is worthwhile to withdraw cash occasionally that you will use to cover your purchases. Give your credit cards a break, and start living on what you have.

Whenever you are going out to buy, take out cash that will cover what you want to buy, and leave your credit cards behind. Even if you see something that you like so much, you will not have any means to pay for it. If you take your cards with you, then you may be tempted to use them to pay for what you had not planned to buy. If you are trying to cut back on your spending, that is quite a big setback. If ever you decide to use your credit card, plan for it and have a set out plan on how you are going to offset it.

Track Your Spending

Tracking your spending involves being accountable for every dollar you spend. You do not have to track your big expenses only, but even the smallest ones because they can really add up to a lot as the month rolls on. You may find yourself running out of money, and yet you have been making the smallest of purchases that you considered to be insignificant. Tracking your spending is healthy for your budget because it keeps you knowledgeable about where your money goes, and how important that is. If you can cut back on your daily spending, you will realize you will have cut back significantly on your total spending for the month. The small things we spend on every day without feeling any guilt are the things that give our pockets a hard time.

Improve Your Budgeting

The reason people overspend is they do not have a spending plan. Earlier we discussed how to budget money and how it helps you to plan the use of your money. At the end of the day, you will not be spending money on things that you did not plan for because you have a set guideline to follow.

Not knowing how much you earn per month in total, and how much your expenses add up to, will cause you to spend money recklessly because you think you can afford it. The best way to sensitize yourself to how dangerously you could be living is to put everything down on paper. Only then will you realize that you cannot afford what you thought you could.

When you take note of your expenses, it may be the wake up call you need. You will realize how much you are spending in comparison to how much you should be spending. You, therefore, should consider learning how to budget for your money, and sticking to the set-out budget. It will help you to manage your finances better, and you will hardly ever need debt to keep yourself covered.

Budget for Every Dollar

This sounds off, doesn't it? Well, it really isn't that bad a statement if you know how helpful it is. By budgeting for every dollar, I do not mean that you should spend everything to the last cent. The idea is that you should assign a task to every cent of your money. It could be to cover expenses, savings, and investments. If you do this, you will not be tempted to spend money thoughtlessly by thinking you have money sitting around with no purpose.

You should have small categories on your budget to which you assign money. These categories should cover everything you need and save for those emergencies that were not planned for. You increase your financial awareness by working out what you want your money to do for you. It denies you the chance to feel like you have a lot of money because none of it is lying idle. The easiest way to do this is to automate transfers from your checking account into different accounts so that the money goes where it should before you even touch it.

Set Your Financial Goals

This is a great way to keep yourself motivated. Setting short-term financial goals means you have something you are working to achieve and it will help you to stay on course. Make sure that your financial goals are not mere statements but are quantifiable. Instead of saying,

"I will decrease how much I spend on lunch", you can quantify it by saying, "I will decrease how much I spend on lunch from $300 to $250." It is easier to stick to a goal that is quantified because you can assess how much progress you have made. If not satisfactory, you can try again because making changes to your spending habits is not a one-day job. It will take time, but with continued effort, you will eventually get there.

Watching your spending is a hard thing to do, but it is possible. You will get the urge to spend once in a while, but you can always devise ways to stay true to your course of action if you are really dedicated. After learning how to budget for your money, and having set goals that you need your money to achieve for you, you will have enough motivation to watch your spending at all costs. You will be able to use your money wisely and it will make you a happier person.

For you to be able to cut back on spending, or to avoid recklessly spending your money, you need to identify what causes you to spend. The temptation to spend money always follows us, no matter how hard we try to evade it. With the advent of so many ways to shop, including online shopping, we have a greater job at trying to avoid the spending mistakes that bust our budgets.

The major cause of overspending is not that people are buying overpriced goods, it is that they are buying what they cannot afford. Things will always cost what they cost, but depending on the size of your pocket, you may or may not overspend. You cannot afford the things you buy with the money that could be best saved for emergencies, retirement, or long-term goals.

The Dangers of Overspending

Overspending on pointless things means you will not be able to save or invest. Investing is the order of the day, and if you are not investing, then you will feel left out in the future when you realize how much progress your peers will have made. Let us look at the dangers you could be exposing yourself to by overspending.

You Become Unable to Save

Saving is not done in planning only, but in action. You have to set aside money in real terms to help you in the future. One day you will want to retire from work, but if you have not been saving for retirement then you will be forced to work until you are old. Otherwise, you will not be able to get by. If an emergency comes up, you should be able to look to your savings to help you out. Even when life is going smoothly— and possibly emergency-free—you should save something to keep you afloat in life's quicksand. What will that be if you keep overspending every month? You definitely need to cut it down and have money left to save every month. That is how the life of a financially sharp young adult should be.

Higher Credit Card Balances

High credit card balances can have a big affect on your finances. When all your credit cards are maxed out, you will be forced to live on your actual income, which will not be able to sustain you and your high spending. Besides affecting your credit score, you will be known for late payments and you will experience high interest rates. You will eventually fail to make ends meet. Using your credit cards to get by, overdrafting your checking account, or constantly dipping into savings is a sign that you are overspending. You need to watch that.

It Affects Your Credit Score

Figure 9: Debts affect your credit score.

When you have too much debt, you tend to be late in bill payments, or you may skip them. Paying only the minimum after maxing out your credit can lead to balances (Dayrit, 2020). Credit cards have ceilings to interest rates. Until you settle your balance, you will still incur interest. Credit utilization for each of your credit cards affects your credit score calculation. This takes into account your credit card balance in relation to your credit limit. This means that the credit balance you have in comparison to your credit limit will affect your score. If that becomes the case, you will have a hard time getting a loan or applying for a new credit card because lenders look at your credit score to decide whether or not they can lend to you.

It Affects Your Health

You may be correct in thinking that health issues may trigger financial distress, because yes, paying hospital bills can be a daunting task. It is also the case that the opposite may be true. Financial distress can cause health issues. You can experience bad mood, poor appetite, inability to focus, and high blood pressure. One can skip out on getting proper health care if their overspending depletes their funds even for basic needs. Do you know that depending on how you handle your money, even important things like health care may begin to appear unimportant to you?

It Affects Your Career

Overspending can negatively affect your career. As mentioned above, financial distress can result from the mismanagement of funds. This will affect your ability to focus on the work you are supposed to be doing for your employer. Your biggest preoccupation will be trying to figure out how you will settle your debts. It may even affect your self-confidence and ego if your credit issues become known to your colleagues.

The worst that could happen is the garnishment of your wages. This is when payment is deducted from your salary and forwarded to the people you owe by the payroll department. You will find it hard to survive, especially if you have been living lavishly. Your wages will come in very low because of deductions, and at the same time you will not be eligible for more credit. The resulting financial distress can lower your productivity at work and jeopardize your career.

It Ruins Your Relationships

Borrowing money from people and not being able to return it can ruin your relationships. If you borrow from your colleagues and you do not pay back, they may try to follow up initially, but eventually they will give up. Besides spoiling your chances of getting help in the future, it affects your relationship with them deeply.

Debt can go on to fuel unease in couples and increase their likelihood of fighting over money. Many married people can discuss and plan together on anything, but hardly ever sit down to sort out their financial life. Fighting is mostly not good in relationships, especially if the involved parties tend to get used to it. The likelihood that they will fight about issues other than money becomes high.

After reading this book, I wouldn't want you to go on and find yourself stuck in the problems that come from overspending. Being a young person who is wary of the detrimental effects of overspending helps you to watch where your money goes. Being careful with your money helps you to build wealth easier. If you make overspending a habit, your life will stand still and there will be no progress for a long time. You may never realize it until an emergency befalls you or you need to retire but cannot because your financial situation is in shambles. To finish off this chapter, let us look at how you can redeem yourself from a messed-up financial situation.

How to Clear Yourself of Debt

Overspending ultimately leads to debt because you end up looking to funds other than your earned income. Continued borrowing will cause you to sink deeper and deeper into debt. It takes willpower and self-dedication to pull yourself up from the situation and start living a debt-free life.

Pay More Than the Minimum Payment

When you borrow money, there is a stipulated minimum amount you have to pay every month. The longer you take to settle the debt, the longer you are going to have to deal with a messed up financial situation. To redeem yourself faster, try paying in higher than the minimum amount. That will see you settling your debt faster—and at the same time escaping the high interest payments. You must, however, check if your loan charges any prepayment penalties and how high they are. Overall, try to pay back your debts faster and free up some money to start living a financially normal life.

Get a Side Hustle

Earning more money is one way to amplify your effort to bring yourself level with the ground. Everyone has some talent or skill they can monetize. Try to find something that you do after your 9-to-5 job to earn more money for yourself. This can include becoming a virtual assistant, freelancing, babysitting, or anything else you think you are capable of. We have talked about paying in more than the minimum payment to repay debt, but the question of where the money will come from may still remain. It could be the case that unless you earn more income, you will never be able to achieve that. So why wait—work extra hard and make things better for yourself.

Sell Things You Do Not Need

It might pay to take stock of your belongings if you are looking for a way to raise cash quickly. You obviously have things in the house lying idle that you hardly ever use or need. You could sell those extra things and raise money to pay off your debts. You can set up a garage sale. It is old fashioned, but it will work. Alternatively, you can sell through a consignment shop or go online. The extra money will do you a great deal of good in redeeming your financial liberty.

Quit Expensive Habits

You could try anything, from raising more income to paying higher that your minimum amount, but if you do not adjust your spending habits you may be doing yourself more harm than good. To better your situation, find ways to get yourself out of your current debt, and at the same time cut back on your spending and review your expensive taste. We discussed earlier that you should track your small expenses, and the large ones, too. If you can identify a constant spending habit you can do without, quit it. It may be hard, but it will not kill you.

It is commonly said that your life is what you make it. Your financial situation is also what you make it. It is completely possible to take charge of your actions and ensure your financial situation is good. Some things may seem hard because you did not take the time to try them out. Make it a point to live within your means, to manage your debt, and to always ensure you are able to save and invest after every income. That is how wealth is created and accumulated. If you spend everything, then you will always have nothing. Survival should not be your main goal, but the accumulation of wealth. Your survival should, therefore, take up only a certain percentage of your total income—the rest should be saved and invested.

Chapter 6:

The Long-Term

The book has so far discussed saving, budgeting, investment, and how to make good use of your money. This is a lifelong lesson you need in order to turn yourself into a wealthy person. You should be consistent in applying the information you have learned from this book to make yourself a better person financially. This chapter will look at how you can be consistent in your financial ways.

You should set goals for yourself that help you to have something to look forward to and will guide your actions today. A goal, by definition, is the desired outcome that one envisions, plans, and commits to achieve. A financial goal, therefore, becomes an outcome you intend to achieve in the area of your finances.

You should have the ability to see the future the way you want it. Envisioning your future helps you set realistic goals and to act accordingly so that, when the time comes, the goal can be achieved. Having a vision is important. You cannot work for something you do not know, but if you are clear about your intentions, you will stop at nothing to bring your goals to fruition.

Practicing good money habits will also add to the possibility of you achieving your goals.

Get into your car and start driving without a definite place to go. After 24 hours, you'll find yourself 20 minutes from your home because you have just been drifting around. Now, get in your car and set a clear destination on your GPS. You'll notice that it will be easy for you to reach that place. In life, like driving, you can see just 30 or 40 feet away from where you are, but if you set a clear destination on your GPS, you'll eventually get where you want, not necessarily where your eyes can reach.

There is a need to learn the difference between short-term and long-term goals, and you need to know how to budget and save for them. Short-term and long-term goals seem to be self-explanatory but, in most cases, people mix them up. Short-term goals are as simple as your immediate expenses and these are the things you will spend money on within a few months or years. Examples are emergency fund, rentals, credit cards, debt payments, insurance, and personal goods.

Long-term financial goals, on the other hand, are usually your big picture costs; they may take you several years or even decades to achieve. They involve more money and require regular attention, as compared to short-term goals. There is also a need to understand midterm goals, which fall somewhere between short-term goals and long-term goals. These take a few years to achieve—they include buying a car, paying off debt, or saving for a down payment (Schwan, 2018)

In most cases, one is likely to have both short-term and long-term goals to balance things out. You should work towards your goals around your usual expenses and focus on basic needs like food and shelter first. Retirement funds and emergencies are also high priority. You should pay off your debt and then decide how to allocate your money towards your wants and other goals. Earlier on, we discussed the need to determine how much money you can save and spend based on your income. We discussed the use of the 50-30-20 budget calculator as a starting point.

You need to make decisions about where to save your money. For short-term goals, you should keep your money in a place where you can access it quickly. For long-term goals, you can put your money into a savings account or a certificate of deposit with a high interest rate. You will achieve your long-term goals faster. Alternatively, you can invest your money if you do not have plans to use it for at least five years, like if you are setting up a college fund for your young child.

How to Set Financial Goals

We all have an experience of trying to set up goals for something that is financially out of reach at the moment. You need to set specific financial goals and be clear about what it is you want to achieve. You must also be specific about how long it will take and the steps to follow until you achieve. At the end of the day your goals should be specific, measurable, achievable, relevant, and time-related.

You need to teach yourself how to set SMART goals. SMART is an acronym for Specific, Measurable, Attainable, Relevant and Time-related (Fontinelle, 2021). There are questions that you need to answer in setting SMART goals for yourself:

Specific

To set specific goals, you should be able to state exactly what your intentions are. You must know what you want to do like the back of your hand. Find specific answers to these questions.

What: What do I intend to achieve?

Why: State the specific reasons and benefits you expect if you achieve the goal.

Who: Who are you going to work with in achieving the goal?

Where: Where are you going to be working from?

Which: Identify requirements and constraints to the achievement of your goals.

Measurable

The entire goal statement is a measure for the investment, but you can have short-term goals slotted into the bigger picture. Here are some questions for the activity:

- How much money have I made?
- How many objectives that lead to the main goal have I attained?
- Did I achieve the objectives and main goal within the planned time frame?
- What are the indicators that I have attained my goals?

Attainable

Your goals should be well defined so you can achieve them. They, however, should be set in such a way that they stretch you and push you to be a better version of yourself. Ensure you have the relevant knowledge in how to achieve your goals to give them a better chance of being achieved eventually. If you ask yourself whether or not your goals are achievable, you should have a ready answer.

Relevant

You must go through these questions and give yourself honest answers to determine if your goals are relevant or not. This is how you can know if you need to adjust your goals into relevant ones.

- Is this goal worthwhile?
- Is this the right time to be setting this goal?

- Does the goal match my current financial position?
- Am I the right person to do this, or do I need help?
- Is it applicable, given the current economic environment?

Time-Related

Your goals should have a timeframe within which they should be achieved. You cannot invest money and not know what you want it to become in a certain timeframe. If your goals are linked to a certain timeframe, it creates a sense of urgency that pushes you to do everything it takes to achieve the goals. If your goal is time bound, you should answer such questions as:

- When do I start and when should the investment mature?
- What can I do six weeks, six months, and a year or two from now to better the possibility of achieving my financial goals?
- What are my daily targets?

Whether your goals are narrow or far-reaching, you should commit yourself to ensuring that the goals are achieved. To help yourself do so, you can make use of a goal chart. There are a few steps to follow in making a goal chart.

1. You should consider writing down the financial goal. Writing it down means you need to specify everything that makes it a SMART goal, as explained above.

2. You should decide the horizon of your goals. Be sure of whether your goal is short-term, mid-term, or long-term. Create a timeline for the goal. If it is an investment, the timeline should cover from the time of initial investment to the time of maturity of the investment.

3. You need to determine how much money you need to save in order to achieve your goal. Be clear about how you will put the money together and how much it should be at the end of the year.

4. Think of every way that can help you to reach your goal. Anything that contributes to the achievement of the goal should be done. Cutting down expenses, finding additional resources, or creating an extra income source are all helpful ideas. Decide on the best combination of methods to achieve your goal, write them down, and follow them religiously.

Determining, quantifying, and writing down your goals is very important because that is your guideline. The achievement of goals is possible if the owner of the goal has a game plan to follow and has set up a timeline for the achievement of the goal. You cannot expect to run blindly into financial success. You have to think about it now, plan for it the way you want, and ensure you work for it.

Monitor Your Money

After saving and investing your money, the general idea is that it should grow. The money you have today is the same that should bring in more money for you. There are a number of things you can do to monitor your money and to ensure you are part and parcel of the wealth creation process. Many people make the mistake of entrusting professional investors with their money and do not make any follow-ups themselves. This is not healthy for your financial growth. The reason why I explained some of the little things concerning saving and investment in this book is because you need to know everything about how your money is being handled.

Occasionally, you will need to rebalance your portfolio. This is important because it brings your asset allocation back in line. When you invest initially, you have a balanced mix of assets in your portfolio, but over time, the financial environment changes and the portfolio loses its balance. Your investments may change in value and this means that your asset allocation may no longer match your investment goals. You, therefore, need to keep track of the investments to minimize the times of imbalance.

The ability of an investor to regularly monitor an investment is invaluable. By being involved in the process, it exposes the investor to the market fluctuations and flows, and creates a more centered point of view. The investor will more easily understand that a loss is not the end of the world. When you invest your money, you cannot be at peace without the knowledge of what has become of it. Receiving monthly and quarterly reports will give you this peace of mind. If you are a short-term investor, you should check in far more regularly on your investment.

Tracking Your Investments

When you have invested money into stocks and other long-term investments, you need a constant update on how your money is doing. I mentioned earlier that you need to be involved in your investment so you know whether or not you are making money. You will also know when action needs to be taken. The book has not, however, disclosed how exactly you can track your investment. This section will shed light on how to keep yourself updated on each and every movement of your stocks, as often as you want.

Many ways can be engaged to evaluate an investment. One simple way is to study the statements that come through from the custodian to see if you have made or lost money. You can also look at quarterly statements that are sent in by your investment advisor or money manager. You need to be careful, however, not to tamper with your investment every time a report comes through, especially if you do not have knowledge on how to evaluate them properly. On the outlook, it may seem like you are losing money, but those running the investment know better how much time the investment needs to start doing well.

In the world of investment, you must know that you do not lose money until you sell your stock. Many people are tempted to sell their stock whenever it starts declining in returns, but the truth is that as long as you hold the stock it can behave anyhow in relation to changes in the market (Brewer, 2019). You should not make such wrong decisions by not knowing what to expect from the reports that come through, but should rather learn how to see the good side of reports before making a choice.

Here are different ways you can track your investments:

Track Your Investments Online

The easiest way to keep track of your investments is to do it online. You do not need to go to a physical location or meet up with the custodian to get an update. You can do it in the comfort of your own home. If you are working with financial advisors or an asset management group, it is common nowadays to have client portals that allow the clients to track their finances. These portals are powerful tools that have made life easier for clients. Other online portals include mint.com and Morningstar.com where clients can access their ratings online as well as set up online portfolios.

Make Use of Spreadsheets

If you want some more control over your investments, the use of custom spreadsheets is ideal. There are two major choices in this category of tracking tools. You can make use of Microsoft Excel and Google Spreadsheets. Microsoft Excel can be used to track the basis for taxes, as well as to calculate aggregate dividend income. It can even warn you about an ex-dividend date. Google Spreadsheets, on the other hand, is a free online spreadsheet program. It may not be as powerful as Excel, but it does make it easier for you to update your documents automatically with information taken from public finance, such as Yahoo.

Use Software to Track Your Investments

Desktop software offers additional features that are not available with online software. Many investors prefer to have software installed on their local system that allows them to track their investments. There are a number of options for the software. These include Quicken, QuickBooks, and Fund Manager. Quicken is ideal for the typical retail investor. QuickBooks is ideal for accountants and sophisticated investors who have a good appreciation of GAAP. It makes investment tracking easier for them. Fund Manager is the closest there is to professional investment tracking for retail investors. It is very powerful, especially if the investment is in corporate and municipal bonds (Kennon, 2021).

If made use of correctly, these tools can help to keep the investor updated on the performance of their portfolios. It allows the investor to be hands-on and to continuously rebalance their investments because they can access information as, and when, they need it.

Finding a Money Mentor

Many people have benefited from having a mentor. Mentors help in navigating things like career decisions and life choices. You should consider finding a good money mentor to help you in your financial decisions. A money mentor provides you with necessary insight because they probably have been where you are and have been through it all. You can accelerate your own growth by tapping into a mentor's existing knowledge and skills.

Figure 10: Grow with the help of your money mentor.

A money mentor should be someone who has expertise in personal finance. This is someone who is willing to help you with ideas when you need them(Frazier 2020). Here are a few nuggets on how to choose a money mentor for yourself:

They Should Know Their Stuff

The mentor should have an understanding of saving, investment, insurance, and be familiar with various tax laws. They should be licensed and have education in the area of personal finances. You cannot be mentored by someone who does not know the area. It is a waste of time and effort. It is also helpful for you to find someone who has actual financial designations. You will know that the person has gone through what it takes to acquire those designations and is complying with what the authorities require for them to retain the designations.

You Should Be Able to Relate to Them

It is vital for a mentor to be able to know everything about you: how you think, dream, behave, and hope. They should not only listen to you and guide you, but they should know you in such a way that if your actions aren't aligned with your goals, they will know why. They will also guide you freely if you can relate to them because they know how to attend to you without causing you to take offence. You need such a mentor if you are to achieve your financial goals.

You Must Tell Them Exactly What You Need

You need to be open enough to tell your mentor exactly what you want. Be clear with them about what is working for you and what is not. If you are clear about everything with them, you have a better chance of creating a solid relationship. This will also help your mentor know how to deal with you and to keep you on track.

You should be open and honest with them. You must not be afraid to get real. You should not have certain areas of your financial life that you dread to talk about, yet you know they are the gray areas keeping you from growing financially. Do not make excuses to avoid these topics or weigh yourself down with guilt and shame—for example, if you have a big issue with alcoholism that leads you to overspending, talk about it. Being open about it gives you and your mentor a chance to devise a plan that will help you to address the problem.

Finally, to make the whole mentorship process an interesting one for both of you, you need to find someone you trust. Know that your mentor handles your issues with integrity and confidentiality. Your mentor should care about you. They should have high moral and behavioral competence and should uphold integrity. You must freely get clarity on issues you do not understand while your mentor provides you with the insight and advice you need.

Having a mentor is important, but it is not easy. Most people who can mentor you about money are people with money—and such people are usually busy. They are less likely to make time in their busy schedules for free. You need to pay and, sometimes, you might not be able to bear the costs. However, that should not be a hindrance from getting the knowledge you need. You can get mentorship through books, academic courses, and YouTube videos.

Improve Your Personal Finances Continuously

Looking at the long-term, you should continuously improve yourself financially. As you move forward in your journey of wealth creation, there are certain traits you should pick up to sharpen yourself. Over time, your financial life should improve and you should find it easier to manage your money.

You should automate most of your payments—for example, your credit card payments should be automated directly from your bank accounts. Your recurring bill payments should be automated. Automating your payments will make it easier to keep up-to-date with payments expected of you. You should also create an efficient means to store passwords and go paperless in running your financial affairs. It will make things far easier for you.

In the long-term, your sources of income should increase. If you cannot negotiate a pay increase, start a side hustle that will ensure your salary is cushioned by another income stream. You can even rent out a room in your house. All that income counts. You should know that most of the dirty work should be done now to enjoy the benefits tomorrow. Increase your savings and help it all build-up to the achievement of your financial goals.

Tips for Successful Long-Term Investments

In the beginning, it is alright that to start with short-term goals, but in the long-run, you should consider investing long-term. Long-term investments, as explained earlier, are investments you intend to hold for ten years or more. There are a number of long-term investments you can choose to grow your money steadily over time for you to achieve your financial goal.

Making a return on long-term investments requires discipline to hang on to stocks even after they have increased by many multiples. You should avoid clinging to arbitrary rules, and consider a stock on its own merits (Kelly 2020). Here are a few tips that can help you to make the most of your investments in the long-term.

Sell a Loser

When a decline has been projected for a stock, there is no guarantee that it will rebound. You need to be realistic about these poorly performing investments. You may feel like you have failed if you lose your stocks, but there is nothing wrong with realizing investment mistakes and selling the stocks to avoid further loss. If an investment is not showing signs of a rebound, sell it. You cannot afford to keep losing money.

Pick a Strategy and Stick to It

You should avoid swinging between different approaches to investment. This makes you a market timer, and it is quite dangerous to be one because you can, at some point, make big mistakes that will cost you. Consider sticking to your picked-out strategy.

Keep a Long-Term Perspective

You must focus on the future and make informed decisions concerning things that are yet to happen. It is always better to invest based on future potential than past performance. Short-term profits can be very enticing, but looking to the future has more benefits.

Have an Open Mind

You must be willing to learn and take in anything useful from the trading environment. If you are open-minded, you can try out anything and your chances of success are high. You keep up-to-date with market changes and trends that help you to upgrade and rebalance your portfolio to keep it running. Understand other factors that can affect your investment. For example, you must know about taxes, although you should not get to the point of worrying about them. Achieving high returns should be your primary goal, although you should also be on the lookout to minimize tax liability.

Avoid Penny Stocks

Losing your investment, whether a small or a big one, is uncalled for. People tend to make the mistake of thinking that there is less to lose with small stocks than there is with large stocks. A loss is a loss. Do not be comfortable with losses because you think they are small. Small losses consolidated will add up to a big figure. You will find that penny stocks fluctuate more rapidly than large stocks, which tend to be more stable. Invest in large and long-term stock that you can watch closely and have a timeline for. The chances of making a loss becomes low because it can be foreseen and action taken accordingly.

This chapter has touched on a number of aspects that need to be understood by an investor in the long run. Being a young person, you will make mistakes in your journey to wealth creation, but that should not deter you from pressing towards your goal. The most important thing is to have your goals and vision written down, and to ensure that you do everything it takes to achieve your goal. Hard work is key, and self-control in the use of money will work to your advantage.

After investing, it is everyone's desire to see their money doing well. The case may not be the same if the investor does not constantly review their portfolios. You should closely monitor your investment process. You must also ensure that you fuel your wealth creation by working extra hard and creating as many income streams for yourself as possible. Take your time to learn about your money and how the assets you have invested in are traded. You must also learn to use investment monitoring tools so that you can reach your investment online or in the comfort of your home. All these are key to bettering your financial life.

Lastly, remember that the journey to wealth creation is better not walked alone. You need the company of people who motivate you to do better your finances. This chapter has emphasized the need to find a mentor for yourself. You should find someone with enough expertise and experience to help you with your financial choices. A good mentor will help you to overcome bad financial habits like overspending and will also encourage your good habits, like investing.

However, although having a mentor is crucial, the fact remains that if someone commits their way to success and wealth, they have to accept that it's a lonely road. Approximately one in every 100 people are ready to endure the ups and downs that are in the road to success. This is the reason why it's lonely up there. It requires a strong character and thick skin to persist in achieving your goals, and because few people are walking the same road, you will find yourself working alone to be successful. Eventually, you will relate with other successful people.

Conclusion

It really has been an exciting journey writing about how young people can create wealth for themselves starting from a very young age. Some people never realized the value of the early years of their lives until they tried to do something so late that they ran out of time. Time is one important resource that should be well-utilized. Do not wait until later on to start. If you intend to accumulate wealth, the earlier you start, the better. So yes, as young as you are, and with as little income as you have, you are in the best position to start.

In the first chapter the book discussed budgeting at length. It wouldn't be reasonable to talk about good financial management on a personal level without mentioning budgeting. If you are to be good with your money, you need the budget to guide your expenditure. Be aware of how much you earn in the budget period and how much you spend. I would be delighted if anyone who reads and brings this book to action would always have a surplus on their budget. It is very possible. You can cut back on expenses if you find your budget to be tight. The book also mentioned how important it is to follow the 50-30-20 budget rule to ensure proper allocation of funds.

You should make saving a priority. Unless you save, you may not be able to start growing your money. I mentioned that growing your money is like sowing, but if you do not have the seed you cannot sow. You should also ensure that you save before you make any big purchases. Do not rely on your monthly income to make large purchases—you should save up for it. You should also avoid relying on debt to save the day if emergencies come up. You should have an emergency fund set up to cover you when the unexpected happens.

As explained in the second chapter, you can grow your wealth significantly by investing. There is a wide array of assets into which one can invest. You should not wait until you have accumulated a larger sum of money to start investing, but you can start little and grow. There are a number of options you can choose from if you have little money. There really is no excuse for someone not to invest because—if you go online—you can start off with as little as a dollar. You should consider lodging your money in assets that bring you returns over time.

The young investor should also understand how money works. People view money in different ways. The way they value it also differs. You need to have alternative ways to create money for yourself. In order to be successful in life, you also need to learn to isolate your life from the crowd. Crowds can push you to behave in a way that you should not. If your peers are spending money recklessly as if it is of no value to them, you most probably will, too.

You should avoid hanging around people who pressure you to spend money that you should not. If you are saving, be clear about it to your friends so they know to exclude you from activities that cause you to spend more money. The people you spend the most time with are the people who know you best. If your friends are good ones, they will help you to achieve your goals, especially if they are organized themselves.

Avoid spending money on wrong purchases. After careful budgeting, you should stick to it. Your money should always go where it was allocated. Do not be an impulse buyer. Stay away from overspending. It is alright to not have money to buy something and still have savings in your pocket. Not all of your money should cater to your spending needs. You cannot expect to grow if you are always on the negative of your finances. Give your finances a break by making sure you live within your means. Buy using cash and avoid the use of credit cards as much as possible.

In the long-term, you should have developed yourself financially to be running portfolios that have big earnings scheduled. You should not look at things without a vision for the future. The future is made today. See what you want to be in the future and put in the necessary work to get there. Nothing ever beats a person who took time to learn to be smart with their finances at a young age. The earlier you start, the better. You need time to make mistakes—and correct them— before you finally make it. When you are older, you cannot afford to make mistakes and you are hardly ever willing to part with your money if there is a risk of losing it.

You should not waste any time making your money work for you. You work hard for your money, so it should work for you, too. Some people will be forced to work past the retirement age because they did not prepare for it. Set aside money to help you in your old age. Instead of retiring late because you do not have money, you should retire early because you have made enough to sustain yourself and your late life.

Being wise with your mine is the key to peace of mind and a happy life. The harder you work, and the more you earn, the happier you will be. So do not waste any time—start now and prepare the life you want to live in the future. It is said that money answers all things. It is better to worry about other things, not your finances. You have the power to turn things around for yourself and it is up to you to use this power or not.

A human being has so much potential. It is up to them to make use of that potential before they die. People who have failed to accomplish their goals and desires in life did not do so because they had no ability. They had all the potential, but they did not put it to use. Working hard is difficult. You may want to, but if you do not have enough willpower, you will not work hard enough. The greatest motivator you have is yourself. Do not wait for an external force to push you to become what you want to be. Push yourself, because you know yourself best. If you want to, you really can create wealth for yourself from a very young age, and this book will be your companion. All the best!

References

Bagus, P. (2020, February 2). *The quality of money*. Mises Institute. https://mises.org/library/quality-money-0

Brewer, J. (2019, August 14). *Do you really know how your investments are doing?* Forbes. https://www.forbes.com/sites/jbrewer/2019/08/14/do-you-really-know-how-your-investments-are-doing/?sh=5adbceb926ff

Budget 2020: Did you know there are different types of Budget? (2020, February 1). www.businesstoday.in. https://m.businesstoday.in/story/budget-2020-did-you-know-there-are-different-types-of-budget/1/395169.html

Chen, J. (2019). *Investment*. Investopedia. https://www.investopedia.com/terms/i/investment.asp

Cruze, R. (2021, March 1). *How to stop spending money*. Daveramsey.com. https://www.daveramsey.com/blog/the-cure-for-excessive-spending

Elmer, J. (2018, November 29). *Automatic negative thinking: 5 ways to stop these invading thoughts.*

Healthline.
https://www.healthline.com/health/mental-health/stop-automatic-negative-thoughts

Figure 1: Budgeting is important. (2017). *Pixabay.com*.
https://cdn.pixabay.com/photo/2017/09/26/
16/14/savings-2789153_960_720.jpg

Figure 2: You can earn interests from your investments.
(2017).   *Pixabay.com*.
https://cdn.pixabay.com/photo/2017/09/07/
08/54/money-2724241_960_720.jpg

Figure 3: Start investing little money and grow it.
(2016).   *Pixabay.com*.
https://cdn.pixabay.com/photo/2016/08/19/
10/20/money-1604921_960_720.jpg

Figure 4: Online business is viable. (2017). *Pixabay.com*.
https://cdn.pixabay.com/photo/2017/03/13/
17/26/ecommerce-2140603_960_720.jpg

Figure   5:   Money.   (2014).   *Pixabay.com*.
https://cdn.pixabay.com/photo/2014/10/02/
16/28/key-470345_960_720.jpg

Figure 6: Manage your time well. (2017). *Pixabay.com*.
https://cdn.pixabay.com/photo/2017/08/30/
07/56/clock-2696234_960_720.jpg

Figure 7: Half full or half empty? (2014). *Pixabay.com*.
https://cdn.pixabay.com/photo/2014/03/29/
08/46/glass-300558_960_720.jpg

Figure 8: Beware of retail therapy. (2012). *Pixabay.com*.
https://cdn.pixabay.com/photo/2012/05/04/
10/57/consumer-47205_960_720.png

Figure 9: Debts affect your credit score. (2012).
Pixabay.com.
https://cdn.pixabay.com/photo/2012/04/24/
17/56/credit-40671_960_720.png

Figure 10: Grow with the help of your money mentor.
(2017). *Pixabay.com*.
https://cdn.pixabay.com/photo/2017/02/13/
15/55/mentor-2062999_960_720.png

Guina, R. (2019, March 18). *Spend less than you earn - the
key to building wealth*. Cashmoneylife.com.
https://cashmoneylife.com/spend-less-than-
you-earn/

*How to stop spending money: 7 tips and tricks to curb your
overspending*. (n.d.). My Money Coach.
https://www.mymoneycoach.ca/blog/how-to-
stop-spending-money-7-tips.html

Your 6-Step Guide to Making a Personal Budget (2019). The
Balance. https://www.thebalance.com/how-to-
make-a-budget-1289587

Investopedia. (2019). *Money*. Investopedia.
https://www.investopedia.com/terms/m/mon
ey.asp

Johnson, H. (2016, August 21). *Here's what happens when you don't have a budget.* The Simple Dollar. https://www.thesimpledollar.com/save-money/heres-what-happens-when-you-dont-have-a-budget/

Kennon, J. (2021a, January 30). *Is a certificate of deposit or money market account better for you?* The Balance. https://www.thebalance.com/certificates-of-deposit-versus-money-markets-356054

Kennon, J. (2021b, February 10). *The easiest ways to track investments.* The Balance. https://www.thebalance.com/what-are-the-easiest-ways-to-track-my-investments-357627

Schwahn, L. (2018, July 20). *How to budget for short-term and long-term financial goals.* NerdWallet. https://www.nerdwallet.com/article/finance/short-vs-long-term-goals

Sethi, R. (2019, March 15). *I will teach you to be rich.* https://www.iwillteachyoutoberich.com/blog/step-3-to-getting-rich-make-your-money-earn-for-you/

Staff, W. G. (n.d.). *7 reasons to be careful when choosing friends and how to do so.* Wealthy Gorilla. https://wealthygorilla.com/7-reasons-careful-choosing-friends/

Thrive Global. (2019, July 24). *Role of friendship: 10 ways how friends can help you achieve your goals.*

Thriveglobal.com.
https://thriveglobal.com/stories/role-of-friendship-10-ways-how-friends-can-help-you-achieve-your-goals/

Vohwinkle, J. (2009, July 23). *Basic budgeting tips everyone should know.* The Balance. https://www.thebalance.com/budgeting-101-1289589

Weliver, D. (2021, February 11). *6 ways to start investing with little money.* Money under 30. https://www.moneyunder30.com/start-investing-with-little-money

Whiteside, E. (2019). *What is the 50/20/30 budget rule?* Investopedia. https://www.investopedia.com/ask/answers/022916/what-502030-budget-rule.asp

Zeder, R. (2016, September 17). *The four different types of money.* Quickonomics. https://quickonomics.com/different-types-of-money/

Made in the USA
Coppell, TX
29 December 2021

70406644R00077